T jobable of Contents

Liars, Cowards, Quitters & Me

God's Unlikely Recruits

ALLEN REDING

ISBN: 979-8-9958369-0-2

To Becky, the best person I've ever known, and who inexplicably thinks the world of me.

Acknowledgments

I'm tempted to say that writing this—my very first book—has been a solitary endeavor. But after months of researching, writing, editing, and rewriting these words again and again, I know that wouldn't be true.

This book is about how God takes nobodies and uses them to accomplish incredible things. Whether anyone who reads this will think this is one of those things... well, I'll leave that to them. But from where I sit, it's felt like climbing a great mountain.

Okay, not Everest—but still daunting. More like climbing Mt. Rushmore, which I've learned is a federal crime... unless the climbing is metaphorical.

To my Reding and Welch families, and to the vast teacher family I've been blessed to belong to — you believed in me for years, sometimes before I did. Thank you.

I would be remiss if I didn't mention the fascinating research on paleontology and prehistoric marine reptiles supplied by my grandsons, Henry and Liam. Even though none of it made its way into this book, I am deeply proud of both of you.

1

The Teacher and the Terrible Staircase

Imagine sitting in class one morning as your teacher approaches, locks eyes with you, and his face contorts, slowly shifting into a mask of horror and pain.

You hear him say, almost to himself, *oh no, oh no.*

Then, meeting your eyes, he pleads, "Whatever you do, please don't take the stairs when you leave this room. If you do, something very bad is going to happen."

You flash a grin, expecting another joke. But his expression remains unflinching, deadly serious.

"I mean it. Promise me."

You shrug it off. Class happens. Then the bell rings.

You find yourself in the hallway, heading for the familiar staircase. Two steps down, nothing happens, and a laugh bubbles up — until your teacher's haunted face flashes in your mind. The horror. The pain.

You slow your pace. Caution feels harmless. Your hand finds the rail. A few more steps. People stream by, moving in both directions. You squeeze the rail tighter, then tighter still. Halfway down, you notice you're barely moving, knuckles bone-white against the metal.

You take another agonizingly slow step, both hands clamped to the rail.

You almost stop, leaning your full weight on the rail — when suddenly, it rips free from the wall. You tumble down the remaining stairs, the rail still gripped in your hands, clanging behind you like an awful bell.

I used this scenario in class for years to explain something economists call expectations-driven inflation. The textbook version goes something like this: economists predict inflation later in the year, businesses start spending on capital improvements before costs rise, consumers rush to buy homes and cars while prices are still lower, and sellers begin quoting higher prices in anticipation.

Even though the original prediction was completely unfounded, the fact that people believed it and acted on that belief caused the very thing the economists were predicting. The warning created what it warned against.

I always thought of it as a Twilight Zone scenario — and I still do. Rod Serling's signature was that the trap was always built into the premise from the very beginning. Nobody saw it coming because they were too busy trying to escape it.

That's exactly what happens on the staircase. The student doesn't fall because of bad luck or poor judgment. The student falls because of a fear that was reasonable at every single step.

For years, I broke down complex, often head-scratching ideas by reaching for whatever everyday scene was closest at hand. Students would tilt their heads, then laugh or nod when the light came on.

Only later, when person after person mentioned it, did I realize I'd been doing something others found unusual. I see connections that most people walk right past and can lay them out in plain language.

I wish I could say I cultivated the habit. Truth is, I've never been able to shut it off.

I taught economics, with a particular interest in college-level macroeconomics. Very little of it makes instinctive sense the way a textbook presents it, which meant I was never short of work.

Most of my best analogies came to me in the moment I needed them — something in the air of a classroom, a face that told me the explanation wasn't landing, and then a door would open. I'd walk through it, and a minute later, a student who had been lost would lean back in their chair with that look. You know the one.

I took my subject seriously, but I always resisted getting lost in minutia—the kind of detail that never makes it onto a thousand-dollar Jeopardy question. It's not that details don't matter, but they can easily swallow the very thing they're meant to clarify.

Some might say I only see the big picture. I'd argue otherwise. I focus on the big picture the way a four-by-six map of the United States does — there's a world of detail inside that frame.

You won't find North Zulch, Texas, on that map, but here, you'll discover stories about my father, who called it home in the 1920s and 30s.

What I once did with economics, I now try to do with biblical lives. I study, and study, and study — and then I begin to process by talking out loud and recording myself. About half of this book began as voice notes — me working through ideas in real time, just as I once did with a classroom full of students racing the bell.

- - -

One evening, I wandered into the Walmart near home. My wife had given me a rare, short list. While she was at a church event, I lingered, drifting through aisles and electronics before finally filling my cart with frozen spinach, eggs, and other everyday items. After enough aimless wandering, I made my way to the checkout.

That's when I saw Jeffrey.

He looked about twelve, though his height suggested he could be older. Sandy hair draped limply over a pale forehead, framing large, unreadable eyes. His face was long and narrow, a slight overbite hinting he might have once sucked his thumb. The chair beneath him resembled a high-end stroller, only taller and sturdier. He sat perfectly still. No caretaker in sight.

Then, as if someone pressed a hidden button, he began flailing his arms and legs, moaning softly. The sounds were like the muffled protests of a fussy infant. I didn't know what challenges Jeffrey faced. I only knew my heart moved for him — and I looked away.

As I turned away, a woman in the next lane noticed him. Her head snapped back like it was spring-loaded. Her eyes fixed on a tobacco policy sign, her posture going rigid, like someone trying to hold still while a wasp circled.

A quick surge of anger flared at her reaction, then faded into a deep sadness. I had done the same thing. I had looked away too.

In that moment, I had a sudden vision of what life must look like from Jeffrey's chair. The turned heads. The rigid shoulders. The careful management of eye contact. I lowered my head.

God, I prayed under my breath, *please let him know you love him.*

The answer arrived so quickly and clearly it startled me—a calm, steady sentence that settled in my mind as if whispered just behind my ear, nothing like my usual anxious thoughts:

That's why you*'re here.*

By then, my last groceries were bagged. I swiped my card, quietly wishing someone would come for the boy before I finished. No one did.

Then I turned my cart and moved slowly toward him.

I stopped beside him, smiled, and in the most relaxed tone I could manage, I said, "So — what's your name?"

The few seconds I waited felt like an eternity. He didn't move or show any sign he'd heard me. After an awkward pause, I pushed my cart toward the exit and out into the steamy summer night, wondering what lesson I was meant to find in something that felt so completely futile.

Sitting behind the wheel, I couldn't stop thinking about the boy. I still don't know exactly why, but I knew I'd never forget him — and I didn't want him to remain just *that boy in the wheelchair*. He needed a name. He needed a voice. That night in the parking lot, I felt responsible for giving him both. So I called him Jeffrey.

- - -

I don't believe it was an accident that Jeffrey was waiting for me at the end of that slow summer shopping trip. Call it what you will. I believe people cross our paths for a reason.

The people you will read about in these pages arrived in mine.

They were real people with real struggles, real failures, and real loves. They lived twenty, thirty, even forty centuries ago, in a world as foreign to ours as the Flintstones are to the Jetsons. Two families in different realities — one in caves, one in the clouds — and yet at their core, they are the same. The arguments. The longing. The loyalty. The heartbreak. The love. The distance between their world and ours is vast. But the distance between their hearts and ours is not.

It's easy to imagine that people in biblical times had nothing we'd recognize as life. No high-speed internet or instant access to the world's knowledge. No music, no films, no novels to transport them beyond their own time. But I think that's a mistake. Without all the trinkets and distractions of today, maybe the substance of their lives was, in some ways, even greater than ours.

Strip away all the busyness of my own life, and what remains is the story of a young man who met an extraordinary young woman and built a life with her. Sons and daughters.

Grandsons. Shared joys, hopes, sorrows, laughter, and countless moments simply holding each other. That's what truly matters when I'm honest about it.

And I don't believe that on that level our lives are much different from the men and women whose stories are told in scripture.

They are not strangers. They are us, dressed differently, living in a tougher world, but carrying the same hearts.

They are not stained-glass figures or distant monuments. Many of them are Jeffrey—overlooked, misunderstood, reduced to a footnote in someone else's bigger story.

What I have tried to do, the same thing I tried to do every day in a classroom, is slow down long enough to actually look. To find the staircase inside the story.

Hebrews 11:4 says Abel, though long dead, "still speaks."

That's what I believe about all of them. And that's what this book is trying to do: slow down long enough to listen.

To stop my cart. To say a name out loud.

To give someone a voice.

And then to be quiet long enough to hear what they have to say.

2

Noah and the Giant Refrigerator

"Mr. Reding, have you seen it yet?"

Period after period, especially on Mondays, young ladies would burst into my freshman geography classroom, eyes sparkling with excitement, and in time, laced with genuine concern. It was early 1998, a couple of years into my teaching career, and a cultural tidal wave had rattled the world.

Its name was *Titanic*, James Cameron's blockbuster that premiered on December 19, 1997 and like the iceberg that claimed the ship, it hit the world with little warning. The film would go on to gross more than \$2.2 billion worldwide, becoming not just a movie but a phenomenon that dominated conversations everywhere.

My students, mostly teenage girls, had poured their Friday and Saturday nights — and chunks of their parents' hard-earned money — into watching Leonardo DiCaprio go down with the ship, often for the fourth or fifth time.

"Not yet," I'd reply, offering a reassuring smile.

The questions persisted through weeks that stretched into months. *Titanic* was unstoppable, a billion-dollar behemoth everyone was talking about. By week eight, their queries turned incredulous.

It was as if I was deliberately hiding in a bunker buried deep beneath a mountain while the world basked in spring sunshine.

"You still haven't seen it?"

I'd meet their gazes, smile again, and repeat: "I'm going to. Promise."

They believed me — I was their teacher, a man of my word. In their teen world, skipping *Titanic* was inconceivable. Still, at 37, I was behind the times, just a few short steps away from the teenage conception of old age: 40.

Those were transitional years for me, and at the time, I didn't realize how much I was changing. Without a conscious decision, I left behind the psychological need to doggedly pursue pop culture the way Tommy Lee Jones stalked Harrison Ford in *The Fugitive.*

On the other side? Liberation.

I knew nothing of *Jersey Shore* or Puff Daddy, whoever he is — or was — and didn't care. Many peers my age or older could sing along to Backstreet Boys hits and discuss the plotlines of *Dawson's Creek*, something I found curiously amusing. Why bother?

Not me. I was out of step and found I liked it just fine. Fortunately, my beautiful wife felt the same way, preferring Buddy Holly over the manufactured, autotuned hitmakers of the day.

In my off hours, Becky and I shared *Looney Tunes* and *Jonny Quest* cartoons with our kids, all of us camped out on the sofa — at least one kid sucking a thumb despite our best efforts to wean them off it.

As the kids got older, we'd settle in for *The Simpsons* or *King of the Hill* episodes, with antics from Krusty and Dale Gribble busting us up at the same moment.

But all those shows and movies were just background noise compared to what truly mattered. What was the point of raising kids who watched Bogart movies or laughed at the Marx Brothers if they didn't know and love the living God?

They needed to understand that walking with God meant truth wasn't just whatever pop culture declared this week. Godly wisdom endures, while popular truth always has a short expiration date.

That kind of shifting truth might have suited Noah's world, but not the man God had handpicked to rescue it.

If you look at a Texas road map, Interstate 45 runs almost exactly north-northwest from Houston to Dallas. It has a reputation as one of the straightest interstate highways in the nation. And on a state map, that's what it looks like — a clean line from one city to the other.

But get in your car and actually drive it. There are stretches where you're heading east on I-45 North. Sections where the road swings so far west you'd swear you took a wrong exit. If you zoomed in on any five-mile segment, you might not believe it was the same highway that looks so straight from a distance.

"Noah walked with God" looks like that state map. One clean line across a whole life. Righteous. Blameless. Faithful. But no man walks with God for six hundred years without some eastbound miles on a northbound highway. The text doesn't zoom in. It gives us the aerial view — the view that shows Dallas north-northwest of Houston, with a pretty straight shot between them.

But Noah's life played out at ground level. There must have been mornings when his walk with God felt more like standing still. Days when he just stared at the unfinished hull, unable to lift a tool. Seasons when the snarling voices outside seemed more convincing than the quiet God who hadn't spoken since handing over the blueprints.

The Bible calls him righteous. It doesn't call him unwavering.

We grow up thinking of Noah as a bearded guy leading monkeys and giraffes onto a big boat. But the reality was far grittier and more daunting. When God looked at the world in Noah's day, He didn't see a world that had simply wandered away from Him. He saw something far worse — a cancer that would be terminal if not excised.

Genesis puts it plainly: "Now the earth was corrupt in God's sight, and the earth was filled with violence."

That word "violence"—ḥāmās in Hebrew—echoes twice in just three verses. This wasn't the odd misdeed. Every neighbor was a possible enemy; every deal could end in treachery.

Genesis 6:5 says, "every intention of the thoughts of the human heart was only evil continually." Imagine a world where every neighbor could harm you, every deal might be deadly, and each day delivered new cruelty.

"These are the generations of Noah. Noah was a righteous man, blameless in his generation. Noah walked with God" (Genesis 6:9). In a world drowning in violence and constant evil, this brief description marks Noah as strikingly different — a man whose daily life was marked by intimate, obedient fellowship with God rather than the surrounding corruption.

In that environment, Noah "walked with God" — in a world populated with human wolves and vipers.

Then God dropped the shocking news: I'm going to destroy every breathing thing on earth, but you, your family, and a remnant of all the animals will be saved.

Then God unrolled His blueprints for the ark and shared its specs with the man He chose to be the builder.

The scale of it all was overwhelming. Floodwaters would swallow the earth, erasing every living thing. Everything. Yet Noah and his family would stand apart—God was forging a covenant with this one man, and the ark would be their lifeboat.

Picture this in today's world: God shows up at your door with blueprints for an aircraft carrier—over 500 feet long, 85 feet wide, and as tall as a four-story building—and says, "I want you to build this. Right here in your backyard."

To this, you'd blurt out, "B-B-B-But God..."

You'd just stand there, jaw dropped. But God would be right in front of you, radiating calm assurance. He wouldn't be glancing at His watch or second-guessing His choice. He'd simply wait for you to realize that His confidence isn't about your skills—it's about His own character and power.

In that stunned silence, God would raise His hands in a gentle gesture and, with the patience of a loving Father, say, "Don't worry. I'll make sure you have everything you need. Go ahead and get started." He'd give a small wave, tell you to holler when you needed something, and step out, leaving you alone with the impossible blueprints and a backyard full of questions.

When I picture that scene, I don't see ancient shipyards. My mind drifts to a University of Houston classroom in the early 1990s. I was a thirty-something transfer student, clinging to a perfect 4.0 GPA and wrestling with a mountain of anxiety about the future. My U.S. history class—spanning 1914 to 1945—rested entirely on two exams: a midterm and a final.

When the midterm arrived, Professor Mitford handed out a single sheet of paper. The test required me to answer a single question, but what a question. With all its qualifiers and demands, that one question took up nearly half the page. It asked us to account for every major figure, every significant event, and every long-term effect of the First World War and its aftermath.

For ten minutes, I sat paralyzed, icy blood coursing through my veins. That question felt like being dropped in front of a massive refrigerator and told to haul it across the room when I couldn't even get my arms around it. The task seemed hopeless. I was ready to pack up, call my wife from a pay phone, and admit defeat before I'd even started.

But deep inside, the Lord sparked a stubborn hope that pushed back against my defeatism. I looked around at a hundred classmates, heads bent, pens flying. Some didn't seem like serious students, yet there they were, writing away. I was the one with the perfect GPA, and I was the one frozen in place.

Then it hit me: I didn't have to move the whole refrigerator at once. I just needed to write a single sentence. So, after a moment's hesitation, I started with Woodrow Wilson's inauguration in 1913.

Once that first sentence hit the page, the words flowed from my pen. Two hours and forty-five minutes later, I turned in a blue book filled with sixteen pages of answers. Somehow, the refrigerator had made it to the corner.

The next Monday, I walked into class, and my graded blue book was placed before me. With only a little apprehension, I opened the cover to reveal a big red "B+" on the first page and a note that said, "A lot of great information but not as tightly focused as I would have liked."

I couldn't help but laugh at his comment and that sprawling question. I walked out of class changed. The smooth stones I'd gathered in that room had toppled my own Goliath.

I imagine Noah had his own moment of paralysis, staring at those blueprints. But once the shock faded, he probably shrugged and thought, Time to find some trees. Then he picked up his tools and got to work.

One sentence for me. One tree for Noah.

What we see as massive tasks from God are really just a string of smaller steps. From that angle, chopping down a tree and shaping it wasn't so daunting. There was no frantic deadline—God handed Noah blueprints, not a stopwatch. The ark would take as long as it needed, and God was perfectly patient.

And it took a long time. Most scholars place the build within a 100- to 120-year window, depending on how Genesis 6:3 is understood. That's over a century of long obedience in a very public arena.

Imagine it: on day one, the neighbors laugh—"Rain? What's that? We've never seen a storm." Ten years in, the chuckles continue. By year fifty, the jokes have faded, replaced by a steady, biting mockery that never quite goes away.

Every Thanksgiving, I walk past the bakery section and grab a plastic bag of Brown & Serve rolls for $1.39. The cheap ones you have to pull apart before you bake them. My wife and I have eaten on cruise ships with artisan bakers. We've had bread with a crust you need a battle-ax to cut. We know the difference.

But every November, I bypass all of it and buy the same rolls my mother and father put on their table for forty years — because they were feeding a family on a working-class budget, and that's what you did.

Nobody watching me in that grocery aisle would understand why. The better bread is right there. But I walk past it every single year because something in me won't let me stop. It isn't nostalgia. It's identity.

Those rolls aren't bread to me. They're an act of faithfulness to people who shaped me — a yearly declaration that where I came from still matters, even if the world moved on a long time ago.

Noah's neighbors watched him drag timber year after year, just as someone might watch me grab those rolls—bemused, a little pitying, unable to understand why a man clings to something that makes no sense to anyone else.

Noah wasn't alone in building. Genesis says Noah, his wife, his three sons, and their wives all entered the ark together. Eight people. This wasn't just Noah's obedience—it was a family staking everything on one man's encounter with the unseen. They could have walked away, chosen ordinary lives, and neighbors who didn't laugh.

But they didn't. They stayed. And when the moment arrived, they stepped through that door as one.

And then it rained.

After a hundred years of blue skies, after decades of mockery, after a lifetime of trusting what he couldn't see — the first drops fell. Genesis tells us that on the very day Noah and his family entered the ark, all the fountains of the great deep burst forth and the windows of the heavens were opened.

The scoffers who had spent a century laughing weren't laughing now. They pounded on the door—God's door, now firmly closed. But it was too late. The obedience Noah began so long ago had become his family's rescue.

Picture it: Noah inside the ark, listening to the first raindrops drum the roof, feeling the ground tremble as water surged up from below. He looks at his wife, his sons, their wives—the eight who believed when no one else did. Maybe, just then, Noah understood why God had spoken with such calm assurance all those years before.

God had never wavered. He wasn't concerned about schedules, logistics, or what the neighbors thought. From the very start, He knew exactly how the story would end.

Vindication didn't arrive overnight. It came after a lifetime of steady faithfulness. But it came, all the same.

I kept my promise to those girls from my class in '98, though not on any timeline any ninth-grader would recognize. In November 2022—almost twenty-five years after Titanic's tidal wave—I finally sat down and watched it.

By then, those teenage girls had begun to reach the grand old age of forty themselves. If they were crossing into "old age," it seemed only fitting that their teacher finally see what all the fuss was about. I hadn't cared about the movie when Cameron was declaring himself King of the World, but that didn't mean I never wanted to watch—it just meant I'd wait until it was simply a film.

I'd told those girls, "I'm going to. Promise." And I meant it. Some promises just take longer to keep—and not every long wait needs an ark and a century.

I've walked with God for about forty-five years. Sometimes I was more devoted than others. There were seasons when my own lack of faithfulness left me so discouraged that I considered giving up and retreating into the easier shelter of my own conscience.

I tried, but I couldn't walk that foolish road for even a day, no matter how frustrated I was with myself. I couldn't pretend the world was flat when I knew it was round.

So I keep going. Day after day. Some days I feel close to God, some days I don't. But I keep walking. Looking at the lives in the Bible—flawed, stumbling, faithless-on-a-Tuesday people—I've realized God isn't disappointed by my stumbles. He knows exactly who I am. And as I surrender, He remains faithful to use me for His purposes.

Noah built for a hundred years. I've been building for forty-five. Neither of us traveled a perfectly straight road.

But the path still leads north.

3

Moses and the Algorithm's Pitchfork

Twenty-five years ago, I could truly write. Not in the way people flatter themselves, but in a way that even my harshest inner critic—never one for kindness—would revisit my words a year later and be honestly impressed. The kind of admiration you feel when you stumble on a craftsman's work. I always knew it was a gift I didn't deserve.

On Saturday mornings during the school year, I'd rise before six, propped up in bed with a wireless keyboard, watching my words bloom across a 55-inch 4K TV—the only way to outpace my creeping cataracts. These hours were meant for recovery. But the fog of teaching never lifts on Friday; it trails you home like an albatross and lingers in your Monday coffee. Still, I wrote through it. I wrote because something deep inside insisted this was my purpose, and I trusted that feeling the way you trust a truth you can sense but never quite prove.

I'd work through the morning and into the afternoon. I'd read it back. The words landed. The sentences had weight.

Then I'd post it on Facebook and watch it wither. What once felt vibrant and alive soon sagged, like a jack-o-lantern slumping on a porch long after Halloween's magic has faded.

A heart emoji from my wife—always my biggest fan. A handful of supportive comments from scattered family and a few teacher friends. Beyond that, silence. I was preaching to the choir, and even the choir loft felt half empty.

What I didn't realize was that the devil lurked in the algorithm. Facebook had its pitchfork ready before I even hit publish, already deciding who would see my words. A retired teacher writing about faith and family was not what the machine wanted to parade before the world.

Kardashian dating rumors, yes. My stories about God and life, no.

I wasn't failing. I was shouting into a room that kept shrinking around me, the walls closing in while I stood blind in the dark.

So I kept writing, and my words kept vanishing into the void. There was no dramatic laptop slam, no cinematic quitting. It was slower, quieter. Saturday mornings shrank, afternoons slipped away, and one day I realized the fog had swallowed me whole. The equation no longer added up.

I was forty. I could write. And it felt like none of it mattered.

Moses was forty when he killed the Egyptian.

But back up one step. Before Moses swung, he looked left and right, north and south, making sure nobody saw him. He saw an Egyptian beating a Hebrew slave, and something in him said this is what you're supposed to be doing. Not the killing — the leading. The delivering. The stepping between the powerful and the powerless, saying, not here, not while I'm breathing.

The instinct was there; God had baked it into his DNA. But at that point, Moses was acting on pure impulse, untempered by God's wisdom or timing. He killed the Egyptian and buried the body in the sand. Covered his tracks. Thought he was invisible.

He wasn't even close.

The next day, he saw two Hebrews fighting and stepped in to break it up — and the man in the wrong turned on him. "Who made you prince and judge over us? Are you going to kill me like you killed the Egyptian?" The word prince is worth sitting with for a moment. Moses apparently saw himself as something among these people — a man with standing, maybe even a destiny. And the man he tried to help told him in one sentence that nobody had voted for him, nobody wanted him, and oh, by the way, everybody already knew about yesterday.

Word had spread overnight. Moses had looked in every direction and missed something anyway.

Nobody rallied to his defense. Nobody said, finally, someone is doing something. He just stood there with a dead body under the sand and people who didn't want his help or even his presence among them. This wasn't Moses being told to butt out — that would've been discouraging enough. This was a repudiation from his own people, ones he had a heart to serve and lead.

And then it got worse. Pharaoh learned what he had done and tried to have him killed. Moses wasn't weighing his options at that point — he was a wanted man with a death sentence already signed. Midian wasn't a retreat. It was the only place left to go.

So he fled. And he watched sheep for forty years and built a solid, predictable life with a wife, kids, and obscurity. Not terrible, not dramatic — just settled. A man who stopped expecting the thing he once thought was coming and had made an uneasy peace with that.

All the way to Midian, Moses had to be thinking one thing: run. Put distance between yourself and Pharaoh. As far as we know, he had no plan beyond fleeing the Egyptian king and surviving. But at some point, Moses had to stop. He had to sit down, rest and take care of himself for at least a few hours.

And it is at that very moment that God begins to unfold His grace, goodness, and blessings to Moses.

Tired and no doubt thirsty after the journey, Moses sat down beside a well. He saw seven young women coming out to draw water for their father's sheep. But then some jerks showed up and started harassing the girls, which clearly violated Moses's sense of right and wrong. Once again, Moses acted quickly and decisively. He hopped up and single-handedly protected the girls from their harassers, and to top it all off, drew the water out of the well for them.

When the seven daughters came back in record time, their father Reuel was surprised and wanted to know how they'd gotten the water and returned so quickly. That's when they spilled the beans about Moses and his Clint Eastwood Man with No Name routine.

Clearly, Reuel was impressed. And it tells us something about the man that he wanted to show his gratitude and extend hospitality to this stranger whose actions spoke volumes about his character. Maybe even at that point, Reuel was thinking Moses might be good son-in-law material, because he dispatched the girls to invite Moses to dinner.

All because Moses sat down by a well. And all because God is gracious and sovereign.

After helping with the water and having dinner with Reuel and his daughters, Moses decided to stay. And not just stay — he married Reuel's daughter Zipporah and gave Reuel a grandson.

If I were Moses, I'd be thinking, "How in the world is my life going so right after some very confusing times and one extremely bonehead move?"

Have you ever noticed how God's grace and mercy seem so much more vivid in the times when we've really failed? It's like the stars in the sky — they never sparkle and amaze more than on the blackest nights.

At this point, the Bible picks up the remote and hits the fast-forward button. We see Pharaoh die, and the Hebrews are still working under a heavy burden and crying out to God, who hears them and is now ready to act on their behalf.

Then came the day. It was a day just like any other day for Moses, who was out taking care of his father-in-law's flock, looking for a new place for the sheep to graze. The Bible tells us that Moses took his flock far into the wilderness and came to Mount Sinai, the mountain of God.

Now, fires in the wilderness had to be common. Parts of the land would be bone dry, and the smallest spark could set off an inferno. But this fire was ordinary until it wasn't. Fire burns. Brush is consumed. Yet here was a bush blazing hot and not burning up.

As Moses moved closer to the bush, out of the fire, God's voice boomed. "Moses. Moses."

I can just see Moses quickly looking around for the source of those words. They sounded as if they were coming from the fire, but...... Then Moses raises his hand in response to a roll call and says, "I'm right here."

From the fire again comes the voice, telling Moses not to come any closer and to remove his shoes because he was standing on holy ground. After forty years of living in Midian, raising a family and tending flocks, it had to be a Twilight Zone moment. One minute, he's leading his flock into some green grass to eat, and the next moment, there's a burning bush that doesn't burn up and a voice coming from it. Nothing — absolutely nothing — had prepared Moses for this moment when he stood before the God of his forefathers, the God who had rescued his life as a baby, preserved his life when he was on the run, and blessed him greatly during his time in Midian.

No one stands before God with swagger for long.

God doesn't ease into it. He tells Moses that He has seen the suffering of His people in Egypt. He has heard them crying out under their slave masters. He knows their misery. And He is going to do something about it.

Then He says, "So now, go. I am sending you to Pharaoh to bring my people, the Israelites, out of Egypt."

Now you know Moses had to be standing there, mouth wide open. Because in his head every alarm is going off at once — not one at a time, not in any order, just a full containment breach, klaxons and warning lights on every panel.

Every reason he shouldn't be standing here. Every reason this can't work. Every way this ends badly.

He doesn't work through them methodically. He just starts grabbing alarms.

His reaction is perfectly human — the same terror and dread any of us would feel if God showed up and handed us the impossible. But Moses doesn't just stand there trembling. He starts arguing, reaching for every reason this assignment should go to someone else.

A few years back, I told a close friend I thought I was a little like George Costanza. He said, "Allen, you are a *lot* like Costanza."

I've thought about that more than I'd like to admit. Because George isn't just reluctant. He negotiates. He finds angles. He builds a case. He argues his way into corners, then deeper into them. And underneath all of it runs a current that Seinfeld writers understood better than most theologians: George Costanza does not believe he deserves anything good. When good things come his way, he assumes the universe made a clerical error, and he's just waiting, bracing himself, for the correction.

Moses at the burning bush is pure Costanza.

You can almost hear the laugh — short, sharp, disbelieving. Who am I to go to Pharaoh?

God answers him simply. I will be with you. And then He adds: this will be a sign to you — when you have brought the people out of Egypt, you will worship God on this mountain.

If Moses had truly comprehended what that meant, the conversation would have ended right there. OK, Lord — when do we leave? But that's not what happened. And under the circumstances, there's no way Moses was going to diminish God by taking a "big deal" attitude. But deep in his subconscious lived doubts that surfaced as functional unbelief — the kind that says I believe you're God, but I can't believe you mean me.

There's no arguing with that — so Moses changes tracks. I watched teenagers do this for thirty years: when you can't win the argument you're in, you open a different one. What do I tell them when they ask who sent me?

God answers him. Tell them I AM sent you. Tell them the God of Abraham, Isaac, and Jacob has sent you.

With that line of argument closed, Moses jumps to a different tack — but with every objection, his voice is getting shakier, more desperate. What if they don't believe me? What if they say the Lord didn't appear to you?

God doesn't give him a short answer this time. He gives him a demonstration. Throw your staff on the ground. Moses does, and it becomes a snake — and Moses runs from it. God tells him to grab it by the tail, and when he does, it's a staff again. Now put your hand inside your cloak. He pulls it out, and it's leprous — white as snow. Put it back. He does, and the skin is restored. And if those two signs aren't enough, God says, take water from the Nile, pour it on dry ground, and it will turn to blood.

Moses is grasping at straws now. I'm not eloquent. I'm slow of speech. I've never been a good speaker. But this is a man who grew up in Pharaoh's court, educated as Egyptian royalty. A man who at forty strode into a fight between two Hebrews and tried to settle it on the spot. Neither of those is a man who struggled to find words. This is desperation talking.

God doesn't remind Moses of his education. It wouldn't be his privileged upbringing or Egyptian schooling that made him a voice for God. Instead, God tells him something far bigger: Who gave human beings their mouths? I will help you speak. I will teach you what to say. The power and intellect behind Moses's words were never his own.

"Lord, please," he begs — perhaps on his knees and with tears rolling down his cheeks. "Send someone else."

That's not humility. Humility doesn't keep finding new angles. That's a man who spent forty years becoming nobody and cannot make himself believe God hasn't made a terrible mistake.

God doesn't reassign the mission. He accommodates Moses's perceived weakness — He'll send Aaron along to speak — but the call stands. Moses is going to Pharaoh.

And here's what's worth noticing: only at the very end of this exchange does God get angry with Moses. Five objections, each one more desperate than the last, and God answers every single one with reassurance, provision, and a companion for the road. He was remarkably gentle with this frightened man. Because as Scripture tells us, He knows we are dust.

Every loving parent has had this conversation. A child overwhelmed with fear, convinced they can't do the thing in front of them, and you don't scold them for being afraid. You kneel down, you answer their questions one at a time, and you tell them you'll be right there with them. If you've been that parent — or if you were that child — you already know exactly what God was doing at the bush.

The story of Moses, like the stories of Peter, Paul, Ruth, and countless others in Scripture, is a case study in how God makes a man or woman of faith. Not all at once. Not by removing the fear. But by meeting them inside it. And many of us today could say the same — that God molded and changed us gradually, sometimes agonizingly slowly, into believers who can stand in the kind of faith we once thought was reserved for people in the Bible.

And then God says something that would have stopped me cold.

Remember what God told Moses right at the start — this will be a sign to you. Read that slowly.

The sign that God actually sent Moses — the confirmation that this was real and not some story Moses told himself in the desert — is waiting on the other side of obedience. Not before. Not during. After. When you're standing on this mountain with the people you freed. Then you'll know.

Moses wanted a sign before he moved. God said the sign is a destination, not a departure gate.

The only thing Moses gets before he takes a single step is a name. I AM sent you. That's the whole advance package. Not a preview. Not a guarantee. A name.

Now go.

Somewhere between that mountain and Egypt, something changes in Moses. The reluctance dies. A man who spent the burning bush looking for the exit becomes the man standing between two million people and the life they left behind. He doesn't stop being human — the fury at the golden calf makes sure of that. But the negotiating stops. He crosses over and becomes the thing God was to him at the bush — the steady voice asking frightened people to trust what they cannot yet see.

It doesn't take long before he needs to be exactly that.

The Hebrews are standing at the edge of the Red Sea with the Egyptian army at their backs, and they do to Moses exactly what Moses did to God.

Were there no graves in Egypt? Did you bring us out here to die in the desert?

Same exhausted reluctance. Same plea to please just send us back. The same inability to believe the man standing in front of them hasn't made a catastrophic mistake.

Moses doesn't argue with them the way he argued with God. He says stand still and watch.

He's been to the bush. He's watched ten plagues dismantle the most powerful nation on earth one by one. He's seen the Hebrews walk out of Egypt carrying the gold and silver of their former masters — plundering the Egyptians on the way out the door, just as God said they would. He has watched every objection he raised at that bush get answered not with words but with events.

The Hebrews had followed instructions they didn't fully understand and watched them work. They believed God must've done something. But they'd been inside their houses for the worst of it. They hadn't stood before Pharaoh. They hadn't watched the Nile turn to blood.

Moses did.

He knows something they don't know yet — that the sign is on the other side of the obedience, not before it.

Stand still and watch.

I know something about standing at the bush.... A year ago, the idea of writing a book felt like being dropped in the cockpit of a 787 and told to fly it. I could barely sustain a 2,000-word blog post. A book — 150,000 words, chapter after chapter, with a common thread running through all of them. I was afraid the frustration would darken my mood and my mind. I didn't even have an idea yet. I just had the nagging sense that I was supposed to be doing something I couldn't do.

Then, about a month ago, the idea arrived. God asks ordinary people to do extraordinary things. Noah came to mind first — a man completely in step with God and completely out of step with the world. And God brought me the Titanic story, and the chapter came together. Then Ananias, and the AP classroom, and the terror of accepting something I wanted to run from. Then the next chapter. Then the next.

Not one of them came all at once. Not one of them was easy. But each one that came together was a sign — the same kind of sign God gave Moses on the road between the bush and the mountain. Not the ultimate confirmation. Just enough proof to keep going. Enough to turn the page and start the next one.

I started this project as a trembling man before the bush. I believe you're God, but I can't believe you mean me. And chapter by chapter, God has answered that the same way He answered Moses — not with a preview of the finished book, but with the next assignment and the quiet insistence that He would be with me.

The ultimate sign, I suppose, will be the day this book is published and I start hearing from people who were called to big things they didn't think they could do and found encouragement in these pages. That's a wonderful thought. But I've still got a vast Red Sea to cross in this journey.

Stand still and watch.

4

Elijah and the Thin Red Puddle

Last night I made a Whataburger run, returning triumphantly with burgers and fries for dinner. And, true to form, I forgot the ketchup. Again.

So I started digging through our twin refrigerators and unearthed a squeeze bottle with that unmistakable, hollow, mostly-air heft—the kind that spells trouble.

I know, this is the definition of a first-world problem. A man with Whataburger fries and a ketchup crisis is not exactly suffering. I get it.

But I persevered.

I flipped the bottle upside down and drummed it against the counter half a dozen times, trying to coax out every last drop. The first squeeze yielded maybe two tablespoons. I recapped and gave it a few more determined smacks against my palm— another two teaspoons, tops. I could see streaks of ketchup stubbornly clinging to the inside, but a quick mental cost-benefit analysis told me the bottle had won. So I spun around and lobbed it twelve feet toward the trash can.

I missed. The bottle hit the rim, bounced onto the floor, and the cap popped open on impact. What happened next looked like a crime scene.

When I was a kid, I'd have never gotten away with that throw. First, because the bottles were glass, and a miss would have left shards you'd still be finding in six months. But mostly because my father would not have considered that bottle empty. Not even close to empty.

Not Great Depression empty.

My father was born in 1918. Becky's father was born in 1918, too — just weeks apart, as it turns out. Two men who never knew each other as young people, separated by miles and circumstance, both getting shaped by the same hard years into something remarkably similar.

When Becky and I got married, we didn't just join two families. We merged two households that had subscribed to the same propaganda poster from the early days of World War II. Use it up. Wear it out. Make do or do without.

When it came to ketchup, that meant adding a splash of water and shaking the bottle like a maraca. Except it was never just a splash—it was always too much, turning the last remnants into a thin red puddle that barely deserved the name ketchup. Still, it went on the plate. No one complained, though my brothers and I exchanged silent, resigned glances. Where's my calendar

During the last stretch of my teaching career, I found myself thinking about that watered-down ketchup more often than you'd imagine. Because ketchup was never just ketchup—it was a symbol. It stood for a whole philosophy, hammered out in the Depression: if something still had a scrap of usefulness, you squeezed it for all it was worth. You didn't quit. You didn't toss it. You shook, tapped, watered, and kept going.

That meant I wore my brothers' hand-me-down shirts and jackets until the fabric practically voiced its objections. Bath towels stayed in service until you could nearly read the morning paper through them. If something still worked, even barely, it still had a job.

As a kid, I never had to worry about running on fumes. But in the final third of my career, I started to see myself in those last weeks of school the way my father saw that ketchup bottle— threadbare, nearly spent, but with just enough red clinging to the inside to keep going.

By May, after my students finished their AP exams, I was past empty. I was the bottle after the cap bursts off and ketchup splatters everywhere. No amount of water could coax anything more from me. I was exhausted in a way sleep couldn't touch— foggy, like a London day so thick you wonder if the sun remembers you at all.

Beneath that exhaustion was something deeper than tiredness. It wasn't just a need to rest. It was a need to vanish—to board a cruise ship bound for somewhere warm, where the locals greet you with a real smile and a genuine 'no worries, mon.'

Sometimes, in late May, I'd wander into a colleague's classroom and catch them quietly scrolling through job listings. Not teaching jobs—any jobs. I understood. I looked, too. The fantasy of marching into the principal's office and announcing I quit was more tempting than most people would ever guess.

Most of us stayed. Not because we didn't want to leave, but because we needed more than a weekend. We needed a break that seeped into our bones—a break from sleep deprivation, from stress that clings even after you leave the building, from the sense that we were finished. And not just finished for the year.

But that bone-deep, nothing-left, I am done feeling isn't reserved for burned-out teachers. New mothers pacing the floor at 3 a.m. with a colicky baby know it. Generations of soldiers in wartime knew it. Migrant farm workers, backs aching as they struggle to feed their families, know it. Doctors and nurses in the darkest hours of the Covid outbreak knew it. This wasn't just tired or stressed or stretched thin. They were done.

And some took that feeling to the extreme: they were not just done with a job, they were done with life.

That feeling isn't new. It's ancient, and it speaks.

In 1 Kings, the prophet Elijah felt he had come to his supposed end. "I have had enough, Lord," he said. "Take my life, for I am no better than my ancestors who have already died."

Elijah was a prophet in ancient Israel, a man through whom God spoke to a nation that had traded their Rescuer for useless idols. This was the same Elijah who once challenged hundreds of false prophets to a showdown on Mount Carmel, called down fire from the sky, then supervised their execution before outrunning a chariot in a rainstorm. He was fearless, blunt, and his faith in God bordered on the dramatic.

Yet here we find him—a wheezing, empty ketchup bottle of a man—collapsed under a desert bush, alone, begging God to let him die.

Anyone who has limped through defeat and utter exhaustion can recognize Elijah's desperate plea. But what's striking is what led him to that moment.

Elijah's entrance in Scripture is almost jarring. There's no introduction, no backstory, no family lineage, the way most biblical figures get. He simply appears before King Ahab and delivers one of the most audacious announcements in the Old Testament — there will be no rain in Israel except at my word. Then he's gone.

God immediately sent him to Kerith Valley. No one knows exactly where it was, but the place was all sheer cliffs and narrow valley floors—dramatic, isolated, silent country. In heavy rains, water would rush through, but most of the year, the valleys were bone dry. Especially now, since Elijah had just declared the rain was stopping.

I think there were two things happening when God sent Elijah away immediately after his announcement. The first was theological. God was withdrawing His voice from the scene, letting Israel feel the silence of the God they had ignored. Ahab and the people of Israel had given themselves over to Baal and Asherah, and God was essentially saying — Fine. You believe in this god? Let's leave you with him and see how that works out. The drought wasn't just punishment. It was an extended, agonizing demonstration that Baal couldn't do a single thing about it.

The second thing was personal. God was sending Elijah to a place with nothing to do and no one to talk to.

For a mind like mine, always hungry for answers and new ideas, Kerith Valley sounds like a mental coma. No Wi-Fi. No books. No kitchen, no food, no people. Just cliffs, a brook, and the echo of your own thoughts.

But I think that was exactly the point.

God stripped away every distraction. Elijah could wander the valley floor, sit in silence, reflect on his life, and watch the brook shrink day by day as the drought he'd announced took hold. Those receding waters must have sharpened his focus.

God wasn't about to waste that solitude. He would use it—to teach, to strengthen, to shape Elijah for what came next. And when the brook finally ran dry, God would send him on to his next chapter.

To a widow with almost nothing left.

The brook dried up. The ravens punched out. When God told Elijah to go to Zarephath, he didn't need much persuading.

The command was direct. Go at once to Zarephath in the region of Sidon and stay there. I have directed a widow there to supply you with food. No debate, no extended negotiation.

Elijah had just spent a long stretch alone in a valley watching his water supply slowly disappear, eating whatever the ravens decided to bring him that day. A widow in Zarephath sounded like a promotion.

Except it wasn't. Not quite.

Think about it: God didn't send Elijah to a wealthy merchant with overflowing jars and a spare room. He sent him to a widow—someone already teetering on the edge of survival before the drought began. In that world, a widow without a grown son was already living on the razor's edge of poverty. In a famine, she was destitute.

God had just walked Elijah through a semester in Kerith Valley—solitude, dependence, learning to accept provision one improbable day at a time. Now, God was enrolling him in the next course. Same subject. Tougher material.

When Elijah arrived at the city gate, he saw a widow gathering sticks and called out to her. Could she bring him a jar of water? She turned to get it without hesitation. Then he called after her again — could she also bring a small piece of bread?

That gave her pause.

She told him the truth. She had a handful of flour in a jar and a little olive oil in a jug. She was gathering sticks to go home, cook one last meal for herself and her son, and then wait to die. That was the whole plan. There was nothing after it.

And Elijah told her to go ahead and do exactly that — but to make a small loaf for him first and bring it to him before she fed herself and her son.

Today, we'd call that a lot of nerve—a stranger asking for your last meal before you feed your starving child. But the widow didn't protest or argue. She simply did what Elijah asked. That tells you something: God had already been working in her heart before Elijah ever reached the gate. His command wasn't just logistical: I have directed a widow there. He had been preparing her for this moment.

What happened next was the ketchup bottle my father always dreamed of. No matter how much flour she scooped, the jar never emptied. No matter how much oil she poured, the jug still had oil left. Scoop and pour, scoop and pour—it never ran dry.

My father would have stood in that kitchen with a tickled look on his face. I can picture the grin spreading as he witnessed what could only be called God's ultimate thrift hack.

But God wasn't done with this widow. He rarely stops at the headline miracle.

Some time later, her son became sick and died. And in her grief, the widow said something that reveals exactly where she was spiritually when Elijah first showed up. She said — What do you have against me, man of God? Did you come to remind me of my sin and kill my son?

Her view of God was probably as warped as everyone else's in town. She'd lived her life, made her mistakes, and figured God was now settling the score. That's how the gods of her world worked—unpredictable, quick to anger, even quicker to punish.

I imagine Baal worshippers saw the divine the same way: do wrong, suffer for it. Simple, merciless, and empty of grace.

What she didn't know—what she had no way to imagine—was the love, patience, and grace of the God whose prophet stood in her kitchen. The God who kept filling her jar and jug, not because she deserved it, not because her record was spotless, but because He had plans for her that her failures couldn't erase.

She knew Elijah's God was real. She'd watched the flour and oil for months—there was no denying it. But knowing God exists and knowing what He's like are worlds apart. She still pictured Him as a scorekeeper, a debt collector—a bigger, stronger Baal.

Elijah took the boy to his room, stretched himself over the child three times, and cried out to God. The boy's life returned to him. And when Elijah brought him back downstairs and placed him in his mother's arms, something shifted in her that no amount of flour and oil had been able to produce. She said, "Now I know that you are a man of God and that the word of the Lord from your mouth is the truth."

Elijah's God became her own.

Not because the jar stayed full. Because her son walked back through the door.

That was the moment she realized she wasn't dealing with a bigger, angrier Baal. She had been living inside the care of a God who knew her sins, filled her jar anyway, and reached into death to return her son. That's not a God who settles accounts. That's a God who rewrites them.

So what looked like a survival arrangement—God keeping his prophet alive by sending him to a widow with just enough for one more day—was never just that. It was about keeping Elijah alive, yes. But it was also about a boy who would have died, and a woman who would have gone to her grave believing God was her enemy, never realizing He had been her provider all along.

The valley taught Elijah to accept provision from impossible places. The widow's house taught him that God's provision is never just about the one who receives it.

But there was one more lesson coming, and it would arrive on a mountaintop in front of all of Israel. The man who had learned to receive quietly, who had watched flour multiply in a poor woman's kitchen and a dead boy breathe again — that same man was about to stand before the whole nation and call down fire from heaven.

Not long before he collapsed under that broom tree, begging God to let him die, Elijah had stood on Mount Carmel, celebrating the greatest victory of his ministry and one of the most dazzling displays of God's power in all of Scripture.

Elijah laid out the rules himself. Two bulls, two altars, no matches. Baal's prophets would get first pick of the animals and first crack at calling down fire. "You call on the name of your god, and I'll call on the name of the Lord. The God who answers by fire—He is God." And everybody on that mountain agreed that sounded fair enough.

So the prophets of Baal went first. They prepared their bull, laid it out on their altar, and spent the whole morning circling it— shouting, dancing, working themselves into a frenzy in the hope that Baal would answer. When nothing happened, they got more desperate, cutting themselves with swords and spears until blood poured down their bodies.

It's hard not to think Elijah was enjoying himself. In the middle of their frantic, bloody spectacle, he offered some helpful tips: Maybe Baal was deep in thought and needed a moment. Maybe he was busy elsewhere. Maybe he was traveling and couldn't answer the call. Or, just maybe, their god had stepped away to relieve himself and they needed to shout louder.

Pause and picture it: Elijah, standing before 450 desperate, bleeding priests, cracking jokes about their god sitting in a Porta-Potty.

Then Elijah turned serious, fast. He rebuilt the Lord's altar, arranged the sacrifice, and did something that made no sense:

he told them to drench everything with water. Four big jars. Then four more. Then four more again. Soon, water was streaming off the altar and pooling in a trench. Elijah had made his own miracle as impossible as possible—on purpose, in front of everyone.

At the usual hour for the evening sacrifice, Elijah stepped up to that dripping altar and prayed—not a long, flowery prayer, just a clear, direct request: that the Lord, the God of Abraham, Isaac, and Jacob, would make it plain that He alone was God in Israel, that Elijah was His servant, and that all of this had been done at His command so the people would know He was turning their hearts back.

And then it happened. Fire crashed down from heaven and devoured everything—the bull, the wood, the stones, the dust, and every last drop of water.

When the people saw it, they did the only thing that made sense. They fell to the ground, faces in the dirt, shouting, "The Lord—he is God! The Lord is God!"

Elijah didn't let the moment slip away. He ordered the crowd to seize every prophet of Baal, marched them down to the Kishon Valley, and had them all put to death.

Is it just me, or is it strange that after Baal's total defeat and the execution of his prophets, Ahab decides it's lunchtime? The whole kingdom has watched his god humiliated and his religious order wiped out—and the king goes to eat.

After the fire on Carmel, Elijah wasn't finished. While Ahab ate and drank, Elijah climbed back up the mountain, bowed low, and prayed for the rain God had promised. Seven times he sent his servant to look toward the sea; six times, nothing. On the seventh, the servant finally spotted a tiny cloud, no bigger than a man's hand, rising from the water.

That was all Elijah needed. He told his servant to rush to Ahab with a warning: get the chariot moving now, or the rain will bog you down. Minutes later, the sky turned black, the wind howled, and a torrential downpour hammered the plain as Ahab's chariot raced for Jezreel.

Then God turned the scene up another notch. The hand of the Lord came upon Elijah, and he tucked his cloak into his belt and sprinted ahead of the royal chariot, cutting through the storm, outpacing horses and wheels for miles until he reached Jezreel before the king.

When Ahab finally reached Jezreel, he didn't celebrate God's power. He went straight to Jezebel and told her everything — the fire from heaven, the people falling on their faces, the slaughter of her prophets.

Jezebel didn't debate theology or feign awe. She sent a messenger to Elijah with a death threat: by this time tomorrow, she swore by her gods, he'd be as dead as every prophet he had killed.

Some translations of 1 Kings 19:3 say Elijah was afraid and ran. Others use a different word — he *saw,* looked at his situation clearly, and ran for his life. The distinction matters. Fear is something that happens to you. Seeing is something you do. And what Elijah saw in that moment was Jezebel's track record.

After Carmel, Elijah's mind must have been buzzing with what God had done. In those first hours, I doubt he could imagine ever feeling anxious or low again. But then Jezebel's threat arrived, and Elijah knew she meant business. The victory high,

the parade in his mind, the energy of that mountaintop day —
all of it crumbled to gray dust.

What happened next wasn't a memory lapse — Elijah hadn't
forgotten the fire, the rain, or the run. It was a shift in focus.
Overnight, his story stopped being about what God had done
through him and became all about what might now be done to
him.

If you read the "Elijah saw" translation, it looks like a case of
spiritual vertigo. On the mountain, he looked at God, and the
prophets of Baal shrank to nothing. In the desert, he looked at
Jezebel's message, and God seemed to vanish. He was still
seeing through his own eyes — tired, hungry, and fixed on
Jezebel's sword instead of the protection he'd just witnessed.

He even left his servant behind as he plunged deeper into the
wilderness. Maybe it was for the servant's safety, but I suspect
something else: fear and self-absorption were closing in. He
didn't want conversation or company. He wanted to be
miserable and die alone.

Under that broom tree, Elijah was building his own depression
playlist: "They've killed your prophets. I'm the only one left.
I've been zealous, I've done what you asked, and now I'm next."
This wasn't the Elijah who strode into Ahab's court, or the one
who trusted God in the valley and the widow's kitchen, and it
certainly wasn't the Elijah from Mount Carmel.

In the thick of Elijah's self-pity and despair, God sent an angel
who gently tapped him and said, "Get up and eat." It happened
twice, with sleep in between. God didn't start with a lecture or
a list of failures. He started with a hot meal and a nap.

Food keeps showing up in these stories for a reason. It gives us strength, a bit of comfort, and somehow helps us weather bad news and hard days. When Peter had to face Jesus after all his bravado and three denials, Jesus met him on a beach with a charcoal fire and breakfast. "Let's eat," He said, before ever asking, "Do you love me?"

I've done enough funerals to notice the same pattern. People gather, weep, remember—and then they eat. One day it hit me: food is the lubricant of grief. It doesn't erase the loss, but it keeps the gears of our souls from locking up as we try to move forward.

But food and rest weren't the end of Elijah's story. They were just the bridge to what came next. Strengthened by two angel-delivered meals, he journeyed to Horeb, the mountain of God, and found a cave for the night.

There, God asked a simple question: "What are you doing here, Elijah?" Not because He didn't know, but because He wanted Elijah to say it out loud—to name his fear and frustration so they could be faced. Elijah poured out the same speech as under the broom tree—how zealous he'd been, how faithless everyone else was, how alone and hunted he felt.

And what did God do for this empty, frightened man? He didn't send him home in shame. He gave him new instructions: anoint new kings, call and train Elisha, and remember there were still thousands in Israel who hadn't bowed to Baal. The story wasn't over. Elijah wasn't the last faithful one. God's work had never rested on his weary shoulders alone.

Elijah did extraordinary things when he was strong and full of faith. But God also met him when he was finished—when he wanted to quit and die—and still had work for him on the far side of collapse.

That's the resolution to the vertigo. On Carmel he looked at God and the world snapped into focus. In the desert he looked at Jezebel and lost it again. But at Horeb, God didn't restore his confidence by putting on another display. He restored it with bread, sleep, a question, and a road. Which tells you something about how God tends to work — less lightning, more lunch.

And when it happened, God didn't give him a pep talk. He gave him sleep, food, and time. Then a question, not a scolding. Then new work and new companionship in Elisha — along with the news that he had never been as alone as he felt. There were seven thousand faithful people he couldn't see. When we feel like the last one standing, it usually means we've lost sight of the rest of the body, not that the rest of the body has disappeared.

When I am the empty ketchup bottle, I tend to push through and keep working. As if turning the bottle upside down and slamming it into my palm is going to make more ketchup come out. And you know, in most cases, it does release a gram or two more — but it's not worth the inflamed hand I'll have the next day. Inevitably, the writing I do when I'm pushing through wouldn't be good enough for a want ad.

But God's answer to the empty bottle was never hit it harder. It was bread and water and sleep under a broom tree, delivered by someone else's hand. And then, only after the bottle had been quietly refilled, a new assignment and a road to walk toward it.

5

Gideon and the Single Bullet Deputy

Growing up in a cracker box home in the eastern suburbs of Houston, our view of the world was defined by television—three network stations and one UHF channel. By monkeying with the rabbit ears, we could get a clear picture on three of them. The fourth carried some of the most popular shows on television, but getting a watchable picture was hopeless. Its signal came in as clearly as if the station were broadcasting from the moon.

Weekday mornings belonged to a handful of cartoons, followed by a parade of game shows. By noon, the screen shifted to daytime dramas, where towering figures of virtue seemed to set the moral compass for the day. These shows laid the groundwork for my early sense of right and wrong, setting the stage for the heroes I'd come to admire.

To me, there was no greater example of that virtue than Gunsmoke's Marshal Matt Dillon. Tall, steady, and just, Dillon kept order in a sometimes raucous cowtown with fairness and good humor. I admired those qualities so deeply that when our first child was born, I named him Matthew, after the strength and justice I saw in Marshal Dillon.

But as the afternoon faded and the sun slid low, the UHF channels unlocked a new universe. These shows sparked laughter and offered a lifeline from a world heavy with war in Vietnam, unrest, and Houston's endless heat. In that golden rerun hour, we didn't find heroes—we found the lovable kooks, misfits, and oddballs.

Chief among them was the legendary Deputy Barney Fife. If Matt Dillon was a strong tower, Barney was a trembling scarecrow. Knotts would play that nervous, puffed-up coward for the rest of his career. My earliest memory of going to the movies is sitting in a theater, laughing at him in The Ghost and Mr. Chicken as he shakes like a leaf when he enters a supposedly haunted house. In Mayberry, Barney would often puff out his chest and portray himself as "mean and dangerous," but we all knew he was a disaster zone held together by a single bullet in his pocket and the steady hand of Sheriff Andy Taylor.

Beside him stood Gomer Pyle—the wide-eyed, earnest gas station attendant who bumbled into the Marines and somehow managed to stay. Gomer never got anything right, but he tried so hard that his good intentions almost made up for everything else.

Growing up, we tend to think of the Matt Dillons of this world when we think of heroes, but the Bible shows us that God has a peculiar habit of choosing the Barneys, Gomers and Gilligans of this world.

When we meet Gideon in Judges, he isn't standing tall like a lawman—he's hiding, threshing wheat in a winepress. Picture someone so scared of being caught, he's frying an egg over a candle in a closet. The winepress, carved from stone for crushing grapes, was the worst place for threshing grain. It was a far cry from heroic tales, but Gideon wasn't worried about doing it right; he was worried about staying alive. After seven years of Midianite raids, the Israelites were reduced to stashing food in caves just to survive. Gideon wasn't foolish or lazy. He was simply scared out of his wits.

And it is to this trembling man, crouching in a hole with a handful of grain, that the Angel of the Lord appears and delivers a line that sounds like a piece of cosmic irony:

"The Lord is with you, mighty warrior."

If Gideon had been drinking, he would have sprayed water everywhere. Mighty warrior? He was the lowest member of the weakest clan, crouched in a hole, botching a job because doing it right would get him killed. This wasn't a Matt Dillon moment. It was pure Barney Fife—defeated, self-aware, and painfully honest about his limits.

It turns out God isn't searching for people who have it all together. He's looking for a Gideon—someone who knows he's empty-handed, so when the impossible happens, there's no mistaking where the power came from.

Gideon's response tells you everything about where he is spiritually. He doesn't say thank you. He doesn't fall on his face. He argues, but like a weakling.

"Pardon me, my lord, but if the Lord is with us, why has all this happened to us? Where are all His wonders that our ancestors told us about? The Lord has abandoned us and given us into the hand of Midian."

That's not a man who doubts God's existence. That's a man convinced God has packed up and left. The stories of the Red Sea, manna, and Jericho were ancient legends to him. What Gideon saw was seven years of Midianites taking everything while God stayed silent.

He believed in God the way many do: as someone who once acted, but has since packed up and gone on vacation.

Then the Lord turned to him and said, "Go in the strength you have and save Israel out of Midian's hand. Am I not sending you?"

Notice what God skips. He doesn't debate Gideon's complaint, explain the seven years, or launch into a lecture on suffering. He simply redirects: You want to know where I've been? I'm right here. And I'm sending you.

Gideon's objection comes fast. He's the weakest member of the weakest clan — he's nobody from nowhere, and he knows it. The least of the least. The bottom of the barrel. Gideon isn't being modest—he's doing math. He has accurately calculated his own insignificance and is presenting it as evidence that God has dialed the wrong number.

God's answer is the same answer He gives every undersized, under-resourced, overwhelmed person He calls: "I will be with you, and you will strike down all the Midianites, leaving none alive."

Gideon asks for a sign. He prepares a young goat and unleavened bread, brings it out, and the angel tells him to place the meat and bread on a rock and pour out the broth. Then the angel touches the tip of his staff to the offering, and fire blazes out of the rock and consumes everything—the meat, the bread, all of it—and the angel vanishes.

That should have been more than enough. Fire bursting from a rock, an angel vanishing in a blink—most of us would be sprinting down the street, shouting the news to anyone who'd listen.

But here's the thing about Gideon—and, if I'm honest, about me too.

A sign doesn't fix what's broken in you. It only proves that God showed up. It doesn't prove you're the man for the job. Gideon watched fire consume that offering, and his first thought wasn't I'm ready. I just saw the angel of the Lord face-to-face, and I'm still alive. He was more afraid of surviving the encounter than he was encouraged by the commission.

That night, God told him to tear down his father's altar to Baal and cut down the Asherah pole beside it. Build a proper altar to the Lord and sacrifice a bull on it using the wood of the Asherah pole as fuel.

Gideon obeyed—but only under the cover of darkness, too scared of his family and neighbors to risk daylight.

And God said nothing about when it happened. He didn't demand a noon spectacle. The job was to tear it down, and Gideon did. God accepted the obedience and never scolded the shaking hands that brought it.

When the townspeople discovered what had happened the next morning and came looking for blood, it was Gideon's own father, Joash, who stepped in front of them. "If Baal really is a god, he can defend himself when someone breaks down his altar." That one sentence defused the mob and gave Gideon a new name—Jerub-Baal, meaning "let Baal contend with him." His father, who had built and maintained that altar, was now defending the son who tore it down. God was already working the hearts of people around Gideon before Gideon had the faith to notice.

Then the Midianites and their allies gathered—a massive coalition camped in the valley—and the Spirit of the Lord came upon Gideon. He blew a trumpet and summoned the tribes.

But before the army assembled, Gideon asked for a sign—not once, but twice. The fleece. Make the fleece wet and the ground dry. God did it. Then Gideon, almost apologetically, asked for the reverse—make the fleece dry and the ground wet. God did that, too.

It's easy to read the fleece as a sign of faithlessness, but I think it's something more specific. Gideon wasn't testing whether God existed — fire had already come from a rock. He was testing whether God really meant *him*. Not whether God was powerful, but whether God was talking to Gideon, about this assignment, right now. That's a different kind of doubt. It's not the doubt of a man who doesn't believe in God. It's the doubt of a man who believes in God but can't fathom why God would be calling his number. The fleece wasn't a test of God's power. It was a test of God's address book.

I recently opened a new account at my credit union. Even though I was logged in and they knew me, they still sent a verification code to my phone before letting me proceed. I'm in no position to judge Gideon for double-checking.

And God answered both times without rebuke. He knew who He was dealing with. He had always known.

In response to his trumpet blast, thirty-two thousand men showed up.

And God said, "That's too many."

Not long ago, you were hiding in a winepress, trying to thresh wheat without wind. Now you're facing 135,000 enemies with a tiny army—and God says it's still too many. I'd have wandered off, muttering to myself. In what universe is 32,000 soldiers too many for a fight like this?

God's logic was precise and devastating: "You have too many men. I cannot deliver Midian into their hands, or Israel would boast against me, saying, 'My own strength has saved me.'"

God wasn't assembling an army. He was crafting a story. And for a story like this, the math has to be impossible—so when victory comes, only God gets the credit.

First cut: Anyone who is afraid can go home. Twenty-two thousand men turned around and left. Two-thirds of his army was gone before breakfast.

Imagine the United States is mobilizing troops for a major conflict. An overwhelming enemy force is massing on the other side. The commanding general steps to the podium and says, "All right, look—we can probably get by with fewer people. Anybody here got a fantasy football draft coming up? Yeah, you better go handle that." That's essentially what God did—except He wasn't joking.

Ten thousand remained. God said still too many.

He took them down to the water and told Gideon to separate them by how they drank. The ones who knelt down and put their faces in the water went home. The ones who cupped water in their hands and lapped it—three hundred men—those were the ones God kept.

Three hundred. Against a combined Midianite force of roughly 135,000. That's 450 to 1. An army the Bible describes as settled in the valley like locusts, their camels as impossible to count as sand on the seashore.

If Gideon's confidence had been growing since the fire on the rock, it just crashed. God had removed every human reason for hope. No numbers, no strategy, no safety net. Just three hundred men and a single promise: God would be with them.

That night, God told Gideon to go down to the camp. And then He added something that tells you exactly how well He knew the man He was sending: "If you are afraid to attack, go down to the camp with your servant Purah and listen to what they are saying. Afterward, you will be encouraged to attack."

God said, "If you are afraid."

God wasn't speculating. He knew Gideon's fear—fear that started in the winepress, flared when the angel appeared and spiked tearing down the altar and grew as his army shrank from thousands to hundreds. Fear wasn't a passing feeling for Gideon; it was the air he breathed.

So God gave him one more thing. Not another fleece or something dramatic like fire falling from the sky. This was something different—something up-close and personal. God told him, "Go and listen."

Gideon and his servant Purah crept down in the dark to the edge of the Midianite camp. And they arrived at exactly the right moment—because God is never early and never late—to hear a soldier telling another soldier about a dream.

A round loaf of barley bread came tumbling into the Midianite camp. It struck the tent with such force that it overturned and collapsed.

His companion answered: "This can be nothing other than the sword of Gideon son of Joash, the Israelite. God has given the Midianites and the whole camp into his hands."

A barley loaf. Not a sword, not a chariot—just a lump of bread.

Barley bread was poor man's bread—the cheapest grain, the food of people who couldn't afford wheat, and that was what knocked down the tent.

Imagine your spouse waking up and saying they dreamed your house was crushed by a Little Debbie snack cake. That was the dream. And its meaning was exactly what Gideon needed.

If God had written a dream specifically to describe what He was about to do with Gideon, He couldn't have been more precise. And of course, He had.

But here's what I think struck Gideon hardest: he heard his own name whispered in fear by the very people he dreaded. The Midianites—those unstoppable raiders—were losing sleep over him. The least of the least, the man hiding in a winepress, was now the nightmare haunting his enemies.

When Gideon heard the dream and its interpretation, he didn't strategize. He didn't ask questions. He didn't request another sign.

I think that's what changed for Gideon at the camp's edge. The God who had lingered in the shadows—behind the fire, the fleece, his father's defense, every shrinking of the army—finally stepped into the light.

And Gideon worshiped the Lord.

Then he went back to the three hundred as a different man and said, "Get up. The Lord has given the Midianite camp into your hands."

Gideon divided his 300 men into three companies of 100 and handed each man the strangest battle kit in military history: a trumpet, a clay jar with a torch hidden inside.

No swords. No shields. No armor. Just noise, darkness, and fire.

Think about what that means for the men holding those jars. You're standing in the dark, outnumbered 450 to 1, and your commanding officer — who was cowering in a winepress trying to thresh a little wheat a few weeks ago — hands you a piece of pottery and a horn and says follow my lead. No sword. No shield. A jar and a horn.

If you had looked into their faces, you wouldn't have seen a group of Rambos and Terminators. You'd have seen day laborers, fast-food workers, store clerks — a bunch of regular guys waiting for a bus to take them to work.

Gideon's instructions were simple. Watch me. When I blow my trumpet, you blow yours. When I smash my jar, you smash yours. Hold the torch in your left hand, the trumpet in your right, and shout.

The shout he gave them was: "For the Lord and for Gideon!"

They reached the edge of the Midianite camp at the beginning of the middle watch — roughly ten o'clock at night, just after the guards had changed. New guards, still adjusting their eyes to the dark. The timing wasn't luck. The God who had arranged the barley loaf dream was also engineering the timing.

Gideon's company blew their trumpets and smashed their jars. Then all 300 did the same — trumpets screaming, clay shattering, torches blazing to life in a ring around the entire camp. 300 fires appeared simultaneously out of total darkness from every direction.

To the Midianites, jolting awake, it looked like an army beyond counting had surrounded them. Every torch looked like a company. Every trumpet sounded like a battalion. The math that didn't work in daylight — 300 against 135,000 — worked perfectly in the dark, because in the dark, God did the math.

The camp exploded into chaos. Men screamed, tripped over each other, grabbed swords, and struck at shadows. In the confusion, the Midianites couldn't tell friend from foe. They turned on each other. The army that had ruled Israel with fear for seven years was now tearing itself apart while Gideon's men simply watched, torches in hand.

Not one of the 300 had to draw a sword, which was a good thing, since none of them were given swords. They held their torches. They blew their trumpets. God handled the war.

The apostle Paul would write centuries later, "We ourselves are like fragile clay jars containing this great treasure."

The surviving Midianites fled — a panicked, disorganized retreat toward the Jordan River. And then something remarkable happened. The tribes who had been cowering in caves and crevices for seven years — Naphtali, Asher, Manasseh — came pouring out to join the pursuit. The victory they hadn't been chosen to start, they were willing to help finish.

Ephraim captured and executed the Midianite commanders, and their heads were brought back to Gideon.

Seven years of Midianite oppression ended in a single night.

And those men—the 300 Gomers standing in that circle—were not the same men who had scooped water days before. They had witnessed God do what numbers, skill, or weapons never could. They arrived as nobodies and left as men who had seen what happens when God takes the field.

That night's picture needed no rabbit ears, no perfect signal. It was fire, clay, and the voice of God—clearer than anything this world can offer.

6

Abram and the Amazing Ice Machine

I still remember sliding into my car on my very first day as a teacher. After Becky and I prayed, I clutched my shiny new briefcase and settled behind the wheel. I turned the key and put it in reverse. Then, a wave of gratitude crashed over me. The realization of how far God had carried me tightened my throat. Before I knew it, tears were streaming down my cheeks.

I was a teacher now. Soon, I'd have a classroom of my own and roll sheets filled with the names of students entrusted to me. It felt like I'd been handed something sacred, and I was determined to honor that gift in everything I did.

That sense of awe and gratitude stayed with me for longer than I expected, coloring my early days as a teacher. However, inevitably, as with all mountaintop moments, that feeling began to fade in the face of the realities that followed.

Teaching is a profession where responsibilities never stop multiplying. Each year, more tasks pile onto teachers' shoulders. Nothing ever seems to come off. Meetings, test prep, and special education paperwork chip away at the precious time I need to actually teach.

After twenty years and three different campuses, I finally landed at a still-sparkling 2-year-old high school. That summer, Becky and I went to check out my freshly assigned classroom. Right across the hall was a sprawling teachers' lounge, and as I stepped inside, my gaze locked onto a gleaming commercial ice machine nestled in the cabinets.

Becky later told me I was so excited that the hair on my arms stood up. My time at that school was the greatest, the hardest, and the most enjoyable teaching experience of my career. It was the pinnacle. It came with unlimited free ice for a man with a legendary thirst.

Those twelve years proved to be a valuable chapter in my teaching journey. Yet, reaching that point came with a price. With each passing year, the job demanded more. The sense of sacred trust I'd felt that first morning in my driveway was gradually buried deeper beneath ever-increasing responsibilities.

There was no single dramatic moment when my calling vanished. Instead, it was a slow, steady piling on—year after year—until some days, I could barely see it at all.

But let me be clear: the feeling faded, but the commitment never did.

If you have ever had a DirecTV satellite dish, you know that when a storm rolls in, the signal gets glitchy. Sometimes it disappears altogether. But the satellite never stops transmitting. It is always up there, always broadcasting. The problem is never the source—it's the interference between you and it. When the weather clears, the signal comes back strong.

This pattern of feeling called, struggling, and relying on faith isn't unique to me—it's also visible in the story of Abraham.

The man who was born Abram grew up worshiping pagan gods, but this was not a disqualification in God's eyes. In fact, when you look across Scripture, the people who have, from a human perspective, disqualified themselves are the only people God uses to carry out His will.

When we look at the most highly regarded people in the world — the great thinkers, the electric speakers and performers, and the businessmen and women with influence and resources — we think, imagine what that person could do for God. But God has never been impressed by the highly esteemed members of society. Instead, He consistently chooses the overlooked nobodies of this world.

When the prophet Samuel came to Jesse's house to anoint God's chosen king, Jesse paraded seven impressive sons in front of him. God rejected all of them. Samuel had to ask, "Are these all the sons you have?" Well, there's the youngest — he's out tending the sheep. Jesse said it the way you'd mention a piece of furniture you forgot was in the garage. The boy nobody thought to bring inside was the one God had chosen.

Abram was that kind of choice.

Genesis 11 doesn't tell us why Terah decided to leave Ur with Abram, Sarai, and Lot. It looks like Terah's idea. However, Acts 7:2–4 tells us God appeared to Abram while he was still in Mesopotamia. This suggests the move was prompted by a divine word. I can tell you from personal experience: God has often put the same idea in both my head and my wife's. Then, when the topic comes up in conversation, the outcome seems a foregone conclusion.

Whatever Terah's motivation for striking out toward Canaan, he got a little over halfway there and decided to settle down in a busy crossroads town known as Haran. He had moved his family in the right direction, but there was a deliberate pause in the journey.

After some years, Terah died there.

After Terah's death, the story's focus shifts to Abram—a man shaped by a pagan past, without notable credentials, and well past the age when most expect their lives to change. It was then that God approached him with these words:

"Go from your country and your kindred and your father's house to the land that I will show you."

And then God made him a staggering promise: He would make Abram into a great nation, bless him, make his name great, and through him bless every family on earth.

Try to imagine absorbing all of that at once. God has just told a 75-year-old man to abandon everything familiar — country, extended family, his father's house — and walk toward a destination He hasn't named yet. And in the same breath, He has promised to build a nation out of him.

God told Abram, "Leave the life you've known and go."

The obvious question is: where am I going?

God's answer was, "To a place I will show you."

Now I don't know about you, but I like to know exactly where I'm going before I take off. I do not wax nostalgic over the days before GPS. Not only do I want to know where I'm going, but I also want to see the options for getting there and, if we're staying overnight, whether the place has a high crime rate. Because if it does, I'm going to book somewhere else.

But Abram went. And going was no small thing.

The Bible tells us that Abram and Sarai, along with all the people they had acquired over the years and all their possessions, set out together. We're not talking about needing a single Atlas Van Lines trailer to haul your furniture, appliances, and clothes. Back then, wealth was livestock—cattle, sheep, goats, donkeys, and camels.

Moving that many living creatures was a major ordeal. You needed grazing places along the way and plenty of water. You probably shouldn't count on moving at anything beyond a slow, deliberate pace. This caravan stretched out, maybe as far as the eye could see. And there wasn't a single Buc-ee's along the way.

But a deliberate pace was fine with God. Abram and company were moving in the right direction — south toward the Negev, walking the land God had promised him. When he arrived in Canaan, he worshiped God at the great oaks of Moreh and built an altar at Bethel, where he called on the name of the Lord.

What happened next brought a new challenge. A famine arose in the land, so Abram journeyed down to Egypt.

Before he ever set foot in Egypt, Abram had a scheme. He looked at Sarai and said, essentially, you're an incredibly beautiful woman. When the Egyptians see you, they're going to say, "This is his wife—let's kill him and take her." So here's what we're going to do. Tell them you're my sister.

Yes, Sarai technically was his half-sister, but that was just a line he used to save his neck. He demoted her. She went from wife to sister in his mouth because sister was the version that kept him alive. And it wasn't impulsive — he had thought this through, weighed the options, and decided his survival was worth more than her safety, her dignity, and her honor.

This is the same man who had worshiped God at the mighty oaks of Moreh and built an altar at Bethel where he called on the name of the Lord. And somehow all of that worship, all of that recognition of God's grace and power, didn't carry over once the road got hard.

He didn't go to God and say, "Lord, would you protect my wife and me in this foreign land?"

Instead, he schemed.

As a husband who has been married for over forty-five years, I cannot imagine handing my wife over to another man's bed just to save my own neck. I also can't imagine how Sarai felt — to have her husband, the man who was supposed to be her protector, hand her over like a business transaction and then get richer from it. A wound like that doesn't heal overnight. That kind of betrayal goes to the foundation of trust in a marriage.

And sure enough, Pharaoh heard about how beautiful she was and snapped her up. And Abram got paid. Sheep, cattle, donkeys, servants — the text lists them all out like a receipt. All it cost him was his wife and his honor.

The Egyptians had their own moral code — one that took adultery seriously enough that a pharaoh who knowingly took another man's wife believed he was jeopardizing his own soul. Abram's scheme didn't just exploit Pharaoh's decency. It exploited his theology.

When Pharaoh found out the truth, his outrage was justified. "What have you done to me? Why didn't you tell me she was your wife?" He sent Abram away like a father dismissing a son who had embarrassed the family. The pagan king had a stricter code about marriage than the man God called. That is not a comfortable picture, and it shouldn't be.

But here's where God shows up. Despite Abram's cowardice, despite the scheming, despite his willingness to sacrifice his wife's virtue to protect himself, God was faithful. He protected Sarai by pouring out diseases on Pharaoh and his household. God didn't wait for Abram to repent. He moved to protect Sarai when the one person who should have been protecting her was counting his new livestock.

God's protection in those circumstances wasn't just about saving Sarai's virtue, as important as that was. It was also a protection of the promise He made to Abram — that he would father a child through Sarai.

Reflecting on Abram's failures, I recognize a similar pattern in myself: I can worship God with passion on Sunday, yet by Monday I find myself falling short.

Several years ago, I had a student I'll call Myra in my senior economics class. Myra's personality was what I call "the classic bad attitude." On the first day of the course, she deposited herself in a seat at the very back of the room. On the occasions when she was in attendance, she remained there, sporting an uncomfortable look and body language that said, in equal measure, "I hate being here" and "leave me alone."

And leave her alone, I did.

It is painful to admit, but I was great at loving the easy kids — the ones with manners, a good work ethic, and a kind heart. I'd go out of my way for them. The difficult ones I left alone.

I had a boy in class one year who was loud, mean, and outright hostile. I wanted him to blend in with the other do-nothings and at least be quiet while he ignored my lessons. Then one day, his assistant principal mentioned the boy's father, a member of a racist biker gang, was doing a long stretch in maximum security. He said it in a wistful tone that surprised me: "The kid never had a chance." He was right. And I hadn't given him one either.

Realizing I was a Pharisee was a gut punch.

It's painful to think of that today. I never got over it completely, but I did change over time. Myra was the jump start to that change.

One day, after an extended absence, Myra surprised me by coming up to my desk and asking if she could come in to do some makeup work. I agreed to help her the next day. When she arrived, she was sporting her usual dour expression and sat in the back of the room, where she began her work in silence.

Despite Myra's presence, I was determined to keep up with my routine. I began sorting through the many papers that littered the top of my desk, but try as I might, I could not ignore the fact that I was not alone in a small classroom that suddenly seemed very large. As the minutes rolled by, I began to sense a palpable tension in the air. Against a surging tide of discomfort and not knowing what to say, I forced the words from my mouth: "So, how are things going for you today?"

As soon as the words came out of my mouth, I realized how stupid they must have sounded. Despite the many days Myra had been in my class, I had no relationship with her and knew nothing about her. Replaying the words in my mind, they sounded like something a disinterested convenience store worker would say to everyone who comes to the counter.

I was hoping for a perfunctory "Fine, thank you," but Myra's response was direct and honest. "Not very well," she said, and her expression matched the statement.

Knowing I could not leave the question unasked in good conscience, I inquired as to what was wrong. I suppose my awkward questions seemed caring and compassionate because this student, with whom I had hardly spoken for weeks, began to pour out the troubles of her life over the next 45 minutes. As the minutes passed, I sensed a split in the veil that separated us, and, for the first time that semester, we were genuinely speaking face to face.

By the end of that conversation, her makeup work sat undone, and scores of ungraded papers still littered my desk, but at that moment, neither mattered to me. Myra had many problems: a broken relationship with her single-parent mother, no permanent home, and no money, but perhaps most tragically, she had no adult in her life to console, encourage, or speak for her. Well, at least not until that day.

I gave Myra the ten dollars I had in my wallet and my cell phone number in case of emergency, but most importantly, I gave her my friendship and concern.

But Myra was a changed person in my class, and so was I. The "leave me alone" expression gave way to a warm smile, and she began participating in class like a different person. I contacted some of her other teachers and tried to look out for her. With a little help, she turned her academic standing around, and that year, Myra became the first person in her family to graduate from high school.

Abram worshiped at Bethel and schemed in Egypt. I was deeply concerned about and helpful to the kids who put forth effort but wasted little time working with Myras, the classroom sleepers and the various miscreants. God used both of us anyway — not because we deserved it, but because He has never once required a clean record before putting someone to work.

Despite all of this rotten behavior — the cowardice, the dishonesty, the willingness to trade his wife's body for profit, the complete failure to trust the God who had called him and blessed him — Abram did not need to be even close to perfect to be used by God. James 2:23 tells us that this man, this schemer who sold his wife to Pharaoh's bed for livestock, was the friend of God.

Not a servant of God. Not chosen by God.

Friend.

If friendship with God required a clean résumé, Abram's application would have gone straight into the trash.

But let's be careful here. None of this means that Abram's actions didn't have consequences. They did. Missteps leave some very sore feet, and the pain from this particular one lasted a long time. What must that road back from Egypt have felt like? What did the silence between Abram and Sarai sound like? A marriage doesn't absorb that kind of wound and bounce back by the next rest stop.

In my first year of teaching, I expected students to show me respect, and if it wasn't given, then I demanded it. And when a student didn't give it, I addressed it right there in front of the class, voice raised, making an example. I thought I was teaching young people to speak to adults the way I'd been taught as a child.

What I was doing was building a wall between the very kids and me I was there to reach. I still shudder at the thought of what some of those students remember about me. But that pain produced a quieter, wiser teacher — one who learned to pull a kid aside, lower his voice, and defuse things privately. That was a small lesson compared to some. But the shape is always the same. When we're in the middle of that pain, we beg God to take it away. And I've learned in my own life that as horrible as the pain can be, and as desperately as you ask for it to be removed, in the long run, the pain is a grace. Because pain teaches us what mountaintop worship never can.

God wasn't just cleaning up Abram's mess. He wasn't simply pardoning a coward. He was forming Abram into the man who could eventually be called a friend. And that process required Egypt. It required the shame of Pharaoh's rebuke. It required the long, quiet walk home with a wife who had every reason to wonder if she could trust him again. The lesson isn't the failure itself. The lesson is what the failure teaches you about who you really are — and who God is, despite your flaws.

When Abram left Egypt, he returned to the altar he had already built between Bethel and Ai and called on the name of the Lord there. Not a new altar — the same one. A man returning to the last place he had been obedient, after a detour he probably shouldn't have taken.

But fear wasn't the only thing that could knock Abram off course. Egypt had exposed what happened when his courage failed. What came next would expose what happened when his patience did.

In the years that followed, Abram showed generosity to Lot, rescued him when eastern kings carried him off, and refused the riches of Sodom — wanting only God to receive credit for his blessings. He settled near the great trees of Mamre at Hebron and built an altar there. Becky and I still live in the same modest house we moved into in 1987. After nearly 40 years, I'm not sure any newer house would ever feel like home. Abram at Mamre feels like that — the wandering finally stopped.

Some time later, God came to Abram in a vision. And what a vision it must have been, because the first thing God says to him is "Don't be afraid." He then delivers one of the most meaningful promises in all the Bible. God tells him, "I am your shield and your very great reward." In that one sentence, He's promising to protect Abram and bless him greatly.

Looking back, I can see that same promise honeycombed through my own life — through the turbulent college years, through the driveway with the brand-new briefcase, through every classroom and every season. It was there, at work, in the sleepless, crying nights and in the great successes.

Then Abram revealed to God the great burden he had carried in his heart for years. What good were all these blessings if he didn't have an heir?

To answer, God led him outside and told him to look up at the stars. It's hard today to understand what Abram saw that night, because we live in a world of artificial light that effectively washes out much of the glory of God's creation. But if you can get miles away from the light pollution, you will see the spectacular light show that Abram took in.

God then promised Abram that he would have more descendants than the stars in the sky. And Scripture tells us Abram believed God, and it was credited to him as righteousness. Think about that — Abram simply took God at His word, and God wiped away Abram's sins of worshiping idols, lying about his wife, and every act that was opposed to God. Abram, in God's eyes, was a righteous man because he believed.

It's the same great exchange the Lord offers sinners today.

It was around this time that Sarai reached a conclusion that plagued the lives of everyone involved, and the consequences of her choice still cloud our world today.

Sarai was now around 80 and had been trying to have a child without success for decades. Despite the promise of descendants from Abram, Sarai must have concluded that God wasn't going to act, or perhaps He was depending on human intervention to make that promise come true.

It's easy to look at Sarai and think what a stupid idea. But no one who has been waiting on God to do something and then decided "God helps those who help themselves" can be too critical of Sarai.

Sarai figured she would hand over her slave girl, Hagar, to share her husband's bed, and through that union, bear a son. Then Sarai would have a family.

It was a culturally acceptable arrangement. Logical. Practical. Sensible.

What could possibly go wrong?

Sarai's plan would, in fact, produce a son — and a catastrophe that hasn't stopped shaking the foundations of the world.

Hagar conceived almost immediately and began looking down on Sarai with thinly veiled contempt. A slave girl was now carrying the heir that the most honored woman in the household could not produce, and she made sure Sarai felt it.

Sarai — who had designed, approved, and implemented the entire arrangement — must have boiled in rage every time Hagar went into her husband, and now she told Abram the whole mess was his fault.

Abram, a man who had faced down kings and walked with God for decades, raised both hands in surrender. He told his wife that Hagar was her servant and she could do whatever she thought was best.

That's Abram punting on first down.

Sarai treated Hagar so harshly that Hagar fled into the desert.

An angel of the Lord found her at a spring and told her to go back, promising that her son would father a great nation of his own. She returned to Abram and Sarai and gave birth to a boy. Abram was 86 years old when he became a father for the first time. He named the boy Ishmael.

It was not the son God had promised. But Abram loved him.

Abram had heard God's voice. He had counted the stars and believed the promise. He had stood before kings and refused to let anyone but God take credit for his blessings. And then his wife handed him a solution to the heir problem, and he went along with it without a word — the same passive silence that cost humanity everything in a perfect garden a long time before.

Now he was sitting in a tent between a resentful wife and a contemptuous slave girl carrying his child. That reminds me of a cabin steward on a Southwest Airlines flight years ago. He introduced himself to the passengers, then cheerfully announced that they would have the pleasure of being served by his ex-wife and his fiancée. Abram's tent had that same energy — except nobody was laughing.

A man who had believed God for the impossible had stopped believing God for this one specific thing — and the consequences were already louder than anything he had faced since Egypt.

Whatever peace Abram had known at Mamre, he wasn't feeling it now.

By the end of Genesis 16, Abram is still living in what must have seemed like a vast plain between God's promise and its fulfillment. Ishmael is here, the tension is real, and nothing about this moment feels settled. But thank God, this is not the end of the story. It is only the last page of Abram's chapter, just before God begins to make him into Abraham.

7

Abraham and the Camel-Smoking Surgeon

In the summer of 1978, I was involved in a serious accident at my parents' house. A door with a strong automatic spring closure had been pushed wide open, and if allowed to close on its own, it would slam against its frame so hard that you could feel the rattle throughout the house. To keep it from slamming, I stuck my left arm out to catch the door frame so it would close softly. But I missed the frame. Instead, my hand caught the glass set in the door. Growing up in that house, I had done that same move countless times, but this day my hand went through the glass — and through the screen on the other side.

My first reaction was annoyance at the shattered glass. But as I twisted my wrist, I noticed a cut—small at first glance, until I turned it further and saw a deep, gaping wound. Suddenly, blood spurted everywhere—on me, on the floor, painting the scene in panic. I was only 18.

I ran outside screaming and panicking. A neighbor saw me and came toward me, not realizing at first what had happened. I was six foot three; he was probably five foot five. I was told later that he knocked me to the ground, had his son call an ambulance, and found some wire to wrap around my upper arm as a makeshift tourniquet. I ended up downtown at Houston's primary trauma hospital — Ben Taub.

After surgery that Sunday night, my family gathered in the waiting room, joined by a close friend, his girlfriend, and her best friend, Becky. Becky and I had barely crossed paths before, but she showed up at the hospital when she heard about my accident. Six months later, on Valentine's Day 1979, I slipped an engagement ring onto her finger. She was just 18, still a high school junior. In June 1980, three weeks after her graduation, we stood together at the altar in our church and exchanged our vows.

I was 20; she was 19. We thought we were grown-ups. But what did we know?

We celebrated our first Christmas as husband and wife, but then Becky showed me a small bump sticking out of her side. You could push it in, and it would come back out. We waited a bit to see if it would go away on its own, but it didn't — in fact, I think it got bigger. She went to the doctor, and he said he wanted to run some tests.

After her 21st birthday in January 1982, she was admitted to a hospital in Houston. Back in those days, it was not uncommon for patients to spend several days in the hospital while tests were run — quite a contrast to today, when people have their appendix removed or undergo minor heart procedures and are sent home the same day. After about four days of testing, the doctors determined that her bump was an ovarian cyst and scheduled surgery. The doctor performing the procedure was a family friend — and, in fact, he was the obstetrician who had delivered Becky back in 1961.

On surgery day, I stayed by Becky's side until they wheeled her away, then found myself in the biggest hospital waiting room I'd ever seen. It was cavernous—big enough to park dozens of cars, with sofas and chairs scattered everywhere. A giant TV, a novelty back then, played classic comedies. I remember two episodes of I Love Lucy running back-to-back as I tried to distract myself.

I sat alone in that vast waiting room. Since the surgery was supposed to be routine, no one else came to wait with me. It was just me—21-year-old Allen—trying and failing to focus on Lucy's antics. Instead, I watched the clock, and when the promised 45 minutes passed, I moved closer to the entrance, my heart rate increasing by the minute.

Five minutes ticked by. Then ten. Then fifteen. My thoughts raced in every direction, but I clung to the idea that this was just a routine procedure—maybe they started late. Each minute stretched longer than the last. Finally, 35 minutes past the expected end, the door swung open.

There was Becky's surgeon. He had been a lively, outgoing man the times I had met him. I had heard that at 60-something years old, he drove a silver Rolls-Royce — not, I think, because he was showing off, but because he had reached the point in life where he could make that splurge, and it said something about his personality. But the man who walked through that door was not outgoing. The first thing I noticed was that his mouth was set in a tight, straight line. He reached up, removed his surgical cap, and said, "It wasn't what we thought it was."

He told me they had removed a tangerine-sized malignant tumor from my wife's abdomen. I had a million questions in my head, but I wasn't grown up enough to ask the ones that mattered most. He did offer a small piece of good news — the tumor had been encapsulated. Had it ruptured, the cancer would have spread throughout her body, but they had checked her extensively while they had her open and found no other cancer. Then his voice dropped slightly. "She's going to need some very specialized care after this."

I didn't know a great deal about cancer, except what I had witnessed watching my mother's sister slowly waste away and die from it. But I knew some of the most common cancer treatments.

I asked the doctor if she was going to need radiation and chemotherapy. He nodded slightly and said she might. He told me he would check on her later that day — then he reached into his pocket, pulled out a cigarette, and lit it. Since I had nothing else to say, he turned and walked away.

Suddenly, that giant waiting room felt more like the Astrodome.

All I could do was reach for the phone. I called my parents first, sharing what little I knew. Then I dialed Becky's parents—a much harder call, since I was speaking about their daughter. Becky's mom promised they'd come as soon as possible.

Somehow, word reached my older brothers. As I waited for Becky to return, my oldest brother appeared, having left work in the middle of the day just to be there. He greeted me with, "How about a hug?"

The rest of that day faded into a blur—except for one vivid moment. Alone while Becky slept, I opened the bedside table and found a gold Gideon's King James Bible. With no idea where to turn, I flipped it open near the middle, and my eyes landed on Psalm 40.

Though I'd grown up in church, my faith had always been more about knowing than trusting. But in that moment, I found myself praying, asking God for help.

Psalm 40 begins: "I waited patiently for the Lord; He inclined to me and heard my cry. He brought me up out of a horrible pit, out of the miry clay, and set my feet on solid ground."

Those first verses worked a quiet miracle. In that dark hour, so young and desperate, all I could do was cry out to God—and somehow, He steadied me. It was a peace beyond anything I could explain.

The morning after surgery, I arrived to relieve Becky's mom, who had stayed by her side all night. I'd planned to break the news to Becky myself, but she told me her mother had already explained everything. For a moment, I felt robbed of my duty—but in truth, her mom's act was a kindness. Becky had been my love for a couple of years, but she'd been her mother's daughter for twenty-one.

Later that afternoon, a sleepy Becky looked at me and asked a question that caught me completely off guard. "Do you think it was the sweetener I've been putting in my tea at restaurants?"

Inwardly, I smiled, though I doubt any of it showed on my face. I just shook my head and told her quietly, no, I didn't think that was it. It's worth noting that it had probably been only a year or two before that when the FDA required cancer warnings on packages containing saccharin, the sugar substitute in so many restaurant sweetener packets at the time. Her mind went to the most ordinary explanation she could find.

She came home a few days later, but we were still waiting — because the pathologists at the hospital had been unable to identify the specific type of cancer she had. The tumor was sent to MD Anderson, one of the top-tier cancer hospitals in the world. We were told they couldn't identify it either. We waited to learn what kind of cancer it was so we would know what kind of treatment lay ahead.

And then the letters from the insurance company started arriving.

The notices said that since my wife's cancer had been a pre-existing condition, they were denying all of our claims — the tens of thousands of dollars in medical costs were going to be entirely on us. We were 21 years old, living on the $6.50 an hour I was making. Now we were looking at the possibility of a lifetime of debt — while still not knowing what kind of cancer my wife had or what it was going to take to fight it.

Abraham knew something about waiting for a phone call that would change everything.

And then one day, at the age of 99, when he least expected it, the Lord appeared to him.

Abraham had been waiting a long time. God had first made him a promise back when he was 75 — that a great nation would come from him, that his descendants would outnumber the stars in the sky. That was a long time ago. At 86, he had a son through Hagar, Sarah's slave — but that was Sarah's idea, a human solution to a divine promise. It seemed obvious that Ishmael wasn't the child God had in mind. But as the years passed and Ishmael grew from a baby to a little boy to a teenager, Abraham had to wonder. Had God forgotten him?

He hadn't.

Most scholars believe the figure who appeared to Abraham that day was Jesus himself, not yet born in Bethlehem, but present, real, and unmistakable. A pre-incarnate visit. And when he spoke, he didn't ease into the conversation. He opened with his identity: "I am the mighty God." Then came the call: "Walk faithfully with me. Live in a way that is pleasing to me." And then, the moment Abraham had been waiting decades to hear: "Now I am going to act on the covenant I made between you and me." And just in case there was any doubt still rattling around in Abraham's mind, God added: "I will greatly increase the number of your descendants."

Abraham's response was immediate and instinctive — he fell flat on his face. That's pretty typical when a human being comes face-to-face with the presence of the Lord. Something in us recognizes we are on holy ground.

Then God did something that signaled just how serious this moment was. He changed Abraham's name. No longer Abram — from this day forward, he would be called Abraham, meaning father of many nations. And if the name change wasn't enough, God began stacking promises on top of promises. Entire nations would come from him. Kings would trace their lineage back to this man. The covenant wouldn't just cover Abraham —

it would extend to every descendant after him, and it would last forever.

Then God said something he would repeat more than once before the conversation was over. It's something any teacher recognizes: when you keep coming back to the same point, it's because that point is the whole ballgame. And what God kept returning to was this: "I will be their God."

Not just Abraham's God. The God of everyone who came after him.

God marked the covenant with circumcision — every male, no exceptions.

Then came what may have been the biggest moment of the entire conversation.

God looked at Abraham and said, "We're not going to call your wife Sarai anymore. Her name is Sarah. And she is going to be blessed." Abraham may have been nodding along up to this point — new name, sure, covenant, absolutely, circumcision, understood. But then God said it plainly: "I am going to give you a son by Sarah. She will be the mother of nations."

And Abraham lost it.

He fell over laughing. Not a polite chuckle — full, can't-catch-your-breath, tears-streaming-down-your-face laughter. In his mind, God had just become the greatest stand-up comedian in history. He's a hundred years old. Sarah is ninety.

Picture it for a moment. You walk into a nursing home — people shuffling down the hallway in pajamas and nightgowns, moving about six inches at a time on walkers. Out in the main room, M*A*S*H reruns are playing on the big TV, and half the room is asleep before Hawkeye delivers the punchline. But down the hall, one couple has snuck back to their room, an 8-track of Barry White is cranked up on the hi-fi they bought in '71, and nine months later, the home purchases its first-ever bassinet. That's Abraham and Sarah. That's what God just said would happen.

In that laughter, we see something important: Abraham had a small view of God. He was reasoning from what he knew, from what he had observed about people and age and biology. He knew old people. He knew old couples. And old couples don't have babies. It had never happened. So he did what a reasonable person might do — he offered God an alternative.

"Lord, why not just bless Ishmael? He's already here. He's already my son. Let him be your child of promise."

It was a practical suggestion. An understandable one, even. But God wasn't interested in the practical solution. He hadn't forgotten Ishmael — he had already told Hagar that her son would father a great nation, and that blessing still stood. But the child of promise was coming through Sarah. And to make sure Abraham understood this wasn't some vague future possibility, God didn't speak of it as something that might happen. He spoke of it as something already decided.

"Your son will be called Isaac. And my covenant will continue through him — and through all his descendants after him."

God had already named the child. As far as he was concerned, Isaac already existed. The only thing left was the calendar.

But here's what I find remarkable. The same man who fell over laughing at the idea of a baby — who literally could not contain himself at the absurdity of what God was describing — got up off the ground and obeyed God's command that very same day. Before the sun went down, Abraham had circumcised every male in his household. Every son, every servant, every foreigner living among them. Including himself, at 99 years old. And including Ishmael, who was thirteen and almost certainly had opinions about the matter.

He didn't wait a week to think it over. He didn't negotiate the terms. God said, "Do this," and Abraham did it — the same afternoon.

That tells us something important, and I think most of us would recognize it in ourselves if we were honest. There's a difference between believing God when he asks us to do something and believing God when he tells us something about our future. Commands are concrete. You can see the next step. Pick up the knife, do the thing, it's done. But promises — especially promises that contradict everything you've ever experienced — those are harder. Those require you to override what your eyes and your logic and your whole life have been telling you.

Abraham could obey a command without hesitation. What he couldn't do — not yet — was believe that the life God had promised him was actually coming. A son, through Sarah, at their age? That wasn't just unlikely. It was impossible. And Abraham knew what impossible looked like.

When someone tells you something that doesn't match the reality you see, laughter is not normally an inappropriate response. Abraham wasn't being defiant when he laughed — he was being human. He looked at the evidence, looked at the promise, and the distance between them was so vast that the only thing that came out was laughter.

But God wasn't offended, and he didn't revise his promise to make it sound more likely. He didn't even correct the laughter. He just repeated himself — calmly, specifically, with a name and a timeline. Your wife, Sarah, will bear you a son. You will call him Isaac. By this time next year.

Sometime after the Lord visited Abraham and promised him a son through his wife, Sarah, three men suddenly appeared before him. It's just a day like any other, and Abraham is sitting in the entrance of his tent trying to keep cool. Scripture tells us that when he looked up and saw the men, his first thought was to show them hospitality.

He offered them water to wash their feet, a place to rest under a tree, and some prime beef and fresh-baked bread. Abraham's hospitality was much more than the courtesy commonly shown to travelers. The text makes clear that one of the three men is identified as the Lord himself, and as with his earlier appearance, many scholars believe this was a pre-incarnate visit from the Son of God.

Years ago, I was at a tire shop, sitting in a small waiting area, passing the time the way we did before iPhones. I was in my thirties, and across from me sat an older man who looked to be in his seventies. With nothing to read except tire ads, I struck up a conversation. As a teacher, I was naturally talkative, and he was friendly and open. We were having a perfectly pleasant conversation — I think I might've been telling him I was getting new tires before we went on a cross-country driving vacation with our kids.

Then he told me about his kids and grandkids, and suddenly his voice broke. He gasped out the words: "I got cancer."

Suddenly, this nice old guy wasn't crying so much as he was battling through a storm of grief.

One second, we were two strangers talking about nothing, and the next, I was looking at a man struggling with fear and his own mortality. Looking back, I can see that God was in the room before either of us knew it. He had turned my eyes and heart toward that man, and I knew exactly what I needed to do.

I told him about the Jesus I knew, the Great Physician — that God can and does heal, and that he should seek God's comfort in prayer in the days ahead.

I told him that I knew God's help was real because my wife Becky had faced cancer twenty-five years before. I was scared to death at the time — I was twenty-one years old, and I didn't know how to handle any of it. But God met us there.

Without thinking, I did something I'd never done before. I knelt down on that scuffed linoleum floor, took the man's hands, and prayed for him. I wasn't praying to a God somewhere far away. I was talking to the God who was in that little waiting room with us. I wasn't offering him a greeting card. I was offering him something I needed in the past and needed every day since.

Abraham didn't know what was walking toward him across that hot afternoon either.

When you check into a Doubletree, they hand you a warm chocolate chip cookie. When you arrive at the Broadmoor at the base of the Colorado Rockies, you're greeted with a handmade chocolate sculpture that, when broken open, reveals an assortment of candies inside. There's a polite welcome, and then there's an extravagant one. Abraham's welcome was the Broadmoor.

The men told Abraham they would return about this time the following year, and when they did, his wife Sarah would have a son. Sarah wasn't part of the conversation, but she was listening from inside the tent — and now it was her turn to laugh. Acknowledging her laughter, they asked Abraham the question that hangs over this entire story:

Is anything too hard for God?

In the time that followed, Abraham stumbled again — fear got the better of him, and he tried to pass Sarah off as his sister, just as he had done years before. But even there, in a failure he should have known better than to repeat, God remained faithful to protect Sarah and preserve His promise.

Abraham and Sarah were blessed by God even though they were thoroughly ordinary humans. She conceived and bore a son, Isaac, just as the Lord had promised.

Abraham was 100, and Sarah was past 90 when Isaac was born. They waited 25 years for what God had promised them, but oh, the joy — the incredible joy they felt as they held their blessed son. Sarah must've laughed and laughed as she played with her son, and it was OK with her that everybody else laughed too.

Even though he was thirteen years old when Isaac was born, Ishmael had nothing but scorn for his father's new son. This was a dark cloud casting a shadow over the joy Sarah knew as Isaac's mother, and she wanted that irritation gone.

But Abraham was very hesitant to send his firstborn son away until God told him that Ishmael and Hagar needed to go.

Looking at it today, it might seem he was sending his child and the mother off to die in the desert, but God had promised that Ishmael would be the father of a great nation, and he had to trust that God would take care of them as He did.

Years pass, and what happy years they had to be for Abraham and Sarah to watch their son grow up and become the young man of promise.

Some scholars believe that what happened next came when Isaac was twelve or thirteen years old. Others believe he could have been much older. Whatever his son's age, life for Abraham had to have a sweetness like one he had never known before. And then the Lord came to Abraham and made what I think of as the most devastating request in all the Bible.

Not only is God's demand unthinkable to a loving father, but it's put in terms that feel like salt in a fresh wound.

Take your son, your only son, whom you love — Isaac — and sacrifice him as a burnt offering.

Oh, the increasing anguish that Abraham had to feel with every additional word from God.

Sitting here, reading those words and picturing the task makes my skin cold and my muscles weak. But Abraham, just like when God said to circumcise everybody, got right to it the next morning.

Abraham cut the wood, loaded the donkey, and brought Isaac and two of his young men with him to a particular mountain in Moriah — one chosen especially by God. Not only was what God asked Abraham to do devastating, but He also designated a location that was a slow three-day journey away. Three days of a living hell. A slow trip, and hours and hours to think about what he was to do, all while walking along with his beloved son.

But mixed with the grief and torment, Abraham had to be thinking about God's promise to him — that it was through Isaac that descendants numbering more than the stars in the sky would come. And so the journey was one of dread, confusion, and hope.

Abraham's words to the two servants he brought along are curious. He told them, "I will go up and worship, and then we will come back to you."

It's clear that Abraham had a handle not only on the awful thing he must do but also on the faithfulness of God. Throughout his life, he had walked with God and seen God move — when Abraham was doing well and when he was acting in fear.

There is a closeness and confidence in God that comes from years and years of following after Him. Of getting to know Him. This is not the caliber of request that God makes of a much younger man who is still stumbling and learning to walk with his God.

Like Jesus carrying His own cross, Abraham laid the wood for the sacrifice on his only son, who carried it up the hill while Abraham carried the fire and the knife.

Isaac had to be terribly confused, because they were clearly going up the mountain to make a sacrifice, but they had no animal. When he asked his father about this, Abraham replied, "The Lord will supply the lamb for the sacrifice."

When they got to the spot, Abraham took the wood and carefully stacked it, then tied up Isaac and laid him on the wood.

Here's the scene. Abraham is ancient in human terms, and here's a young man, strong and full of energy. The only way the scene works is if Isaac volunteers to be bound and placed upon the altar.

Abraham reached out and took the knife. That was all the truth God needed. There was no dramatic plunge, no last-second rescue with the blade an inch from his son's chest. God didn't need to see the knife come down. He had already seen what was in Abraham's heart — and that was enough. Before Abraham could raise his arm, the angel of the Lord called out, "Abraham! Abraham!" The repetition of his name tells you everything about the urgency in that voice.

God knew what was in Abraham's heart before Abraham ever reached for the knife. He knew Abraham would pick it up. The scene on that mountain wasn't staged to prove something to God. It was staged to prove something to Abraham. When he took the knife in his hand, Abraham discovered something about his own faith that he could not have known any other way — that it was absolute.

And I wonder if looking back, that realization shocked him. Because that's how it works — you don't know what's really in your heart until something comes along that forces it into the open.

Looking up, Abraham saw a ram caught in a thicket, which he sacrificed in place of his son.

Whatever that mountain had been called before, to Abraham it was now and forever "The Lord Will Provide." That name, tied to that place, would be a regular reminder — not just of Abraham's faith, but of God's loving provision.

About ten days after she came home, she got the phone call.

The news was nearly unbelievable. What Becky had was an extraordinarily rare form of cancer — so rare that it almost never recurs. She would not need radiation, chemotherapy, or any other cancer treatment. She would simply need checkups every six months to watch for recurrence.

That was an incredible relief for us, but we still faced an enormous medical debt that the insurance company said they wouldn't cover.

Honestly, I didn't care about the debt. Even if it took a lifetime to pay off, I'd do it gladly—with my healthy wife by my side. Every moment together was worth the cost.

We appealed the denial and enlisted our surgeon's help. After he filed some paperwork, the insurance company agreed to cover 80%. That left us with 20%—still a daunting sum on my wages, but far better than the whole bill.

Three weeks later, my boss appeared with payment notices from a second insurance company.

At first, I was baffled. But as we dug into the paperwork, we uncovered something remarkable.

For one week, our company's employees were covered by two major medical policies. The primary policy, which paid 80%, was expiring just as Becky had surgery. The new policy kicked in right as she was admitted.

The new policy picked up the remaining 20%. What began as a total denial turned into both policies covering every cent. In the end, I don't think I paid a single dollar out of pocket.

Becky asked her doctor whether it would be safe for her to get pregnant, because we were ready to start a family. He said to wait about four weeks for her to heal, and then we could try — but he added a caution. "When we found the tumor, we went all through you," he said. "Don't be surprised if your internal organs are a little thrown off. You might be trying for a year before you have any success."

The best medical advice was to wait four weeks. In our great 21-year-old wisdom, we waited two.

About a month later, the pregnancy test came back positive. We were going to have a baby.

What a turnaround.

Now, more than 45 years later, my wife remains healthy, with no recurrence. If this all sounds like a Hallmark movie, I understand. But it's true—every word happened just as I've told it.

And those first verses of Psalm 40 that I found in that Gideon's Bible in a dark hospital room? The third verse turned out to be just as true as the first.

Despite all the ups and downs that came in the years after, God has "put a new song in my mouth, even praise unto our God: many shall see it, and fear, and shall trust in the Lord."

So here is the question that hangs over Abraham's story, and mine, and the one you're living — the same question the Lord asked after hearing a 90-year-old Sarah laughing on the other side of the tent wall:

Is anything too hard for God?

8

Hosea and the White-Knuckle Nights

The day I stepped into my neighborhood Domino's felt like hitting rock bottom.

I was 31 years old.

A father of three.

Behind on my mortgage.

Married to a woman who deserved better.

And down to $12 in cash, with a meager grocery list that would cost more than twice that.

That's how I found myself inside this pizza place, asking for a delivery job. I had run out of options. Every door had slammed shut. Every plan had crumbled. I knew they needed drivers, but a nagging fear haunted me: what if even this place turned me away?

Still, as low as I felt, I couldn't fathom being rejected.

I couldn't have known it then, and I never would have believed it if someone had told me, but stepping through that door became one of the most pivotal choices of my life.

When the Jewish exiles were carried off to Babylon, conquered and hopeless in a foreign land, God spoke through the prophet Jeremiah: "For I know the plans I have for you, declares the LORD, plans to give you hope and a future." Standing in that Domino's, I felt like an exile in my own life. But God had plans I couldn't see yet.

Here's the thing about being a delivery driver, the thing that made this lowly job perfect for me: you get cash tips. Not on every delivery, but enough. And that meant I could walk in the door at the end of a shift with actual money in my pocket — money Becky could use that same day to buy a few groceries.

In those first few days, cash tips weren't just helpful—they were survival itself.

Fourteen dollars and fifty cents in my pocket wasn't much, but for a family used to scraping by, it was everything. It meant a little chicken, some hamburger meat, rice, beans, and a pack of store-brand diapers.

Our kids never realized how close we came to losing it all. That was intentional. They would face grown-up worries soon enough; I refused to let them carry ours before their time.

At first, there was shock—and, if I'm honest, shame—at taking a job I thought was beneath me. Eventually, I stopped dwelling on it, until the day I delivered to someone from church.

The door swung open, and I caught her curious smile as she took in my uniform and the red pizza bag. I handed over the order as quickly as possible and hurried away. It was foolish pride, but it stung all the same.

When business slowed, the delivery drivers gathered around to fold boxes and swap stories.

Most of them were older than me. That surprised me. What surprised me more was that several of them were going to college.

I'd always thought college was for 18-year-olds fresh out of high school, maybe a few years beyond that at most. But these guys were in their 30s, 40s, taking classes at night, working toward degrees. Day after day, I began to learn that college was not the Herculean ordeal I had assumed it was.

They were good people, but none of them struck me as anything other than ordinary.

A wild thought crept in: maybe I could go to college and earn a degree. Who was I kidding? It felt as likely as jogging up Mount Everest.

I had a wife, three kids, and a mortgage that loomed over us. On top of that, I was flat broke.

There were so many obstacles in the way of my going to college, but one by one, God was sliding, shoving, and kicking them out of the way.

One late evening after most of the other drivers had gone home, I was talking to the manager. I don't remember the topic of conversation, but in the middle of it, she blurted out, "It's obvious that you are very intelligent."

Her comment kicked another objection right out from under me. That was not how I thought of myself back then. I'd been out of high school for nearly 15 years, and I assumed the 18-year-olds coming straight from the classroom would be miles ahead of me.

Having taught high school seniors for the last two decades of my career, I now find that fear laughable.

Little by little, what once felt like madness started to seem possible. When I finally shared my dream with Becky, she didn't hesitate. She was all in, promising we'd shoulder the burdens together.

Not everyone shared our optimism. No one said it outright, but you could see the skepticism in their eyes. Even my parents were unusually quiet. A 31-year-old father of three, going to college full-time with no income? Their worry was written all over their faces.

It was a gamble, but when you're already scraping by below the poverty line, what more is there to lose?

A college degree promised a better job and a future where we wouldn't panic every time the summer electric bill arrived or the car broke down.

Things were starting to fall into place, but I still had to prove I could handle the coursework—and figure out how to pay for it.

I sat for the entrance test at the community college—the first exam I'd faced since high school. Most sections went well, but algebra and geometry left me stumped. Still, needing just one remedial class felt like a small win.

I eventually learned that because of our very humble circumstances, I would qualify for the maximum federal Pell grant, which would be enough to cover my tuition, books, and fees.

Once all our concerns were resolved, I enrolled in classes and bought my first backpack.

I showed up on my first day as a 32-year-old freshman.

I figured out pretty quickly that I was a capable student. Between classes, sitting around over coffee, I'd explain concepts we'd just learned. My classmates would say things like, "When you explain it, it makes way more sense than when the professor does."

Hearing that again and again, a new, wild idea took root: maybe I could become a teacher.

But that path meant four more years of scraping by, four years of wondering if we'd lose the house. I wasn't sure my family could endure that long.

I made the Dean's list every semester and entered my senior year with a perfect GPA, but that did nothing to provide for my family. I was proud of my grades, but ashamed of my son's holey jeans.

I took any job I could fit around my classes. We survived—just barely. It was white-knuckle living. The mortgage was always overdue. I tried to stay just one payment behind, but sometimes it slipped to two, almost three. Three meant foreclosure.

Most nights, sleep wouldn't come. I'd wander the dark hallway into the living room, staring at scuffed walls and tarnished doorknobs, haunted by thoughts of losing everything.

I'd stand there and pray, pleading with God for just one more payment—just enough to make it to next month, just enough to keep us afloat.

We scraped by for three and a half years. Then, at last, I graduated and landed a job as a high school teacher.

I could not have done it without Becky. She prayed for me when I panicked — which was often. She calmed me down when, in frustration, I'd throw my algebra book across the room. She held our family together when I was buried in classes and worry.

She never wavered, never complained, and was genuinely proud of what I was doing, even though we were just barely keeping our heads above water.

Looking back on those years, the money problems were the heaviest burden by far — the thing that woke me up at 2 a.m. and followed me through the day. But running underneath all of that was something I didn't talk about much: the shame.

Soffits sagging. Fascia boards cracked and tired. Paint peeling for all the world to see. A widening crack in the front wall made it seem like the house was splitting in two. And there I was, standing on strangers' doorsteps in a Domino's shirt, that ridiculous lighted sign perched on my old car.

Most people wouldn't be bothered by those things, but for me, the shame was real. I wore it like a threadbare, moth-eaten coat. I was painfully aware of my circumstances, even if others weren't. If you've ever carried a shame invisible to everyone else, you know exactly what I mean.

I know the comparison seems absurd — a run-down house and a pizza delivery job versus a divine command to marry a prostitute. But to some people even a little shame is a crushing burden. There was nothing little about the shame that fell on Hosea.

Hosea was a prophet in the 8th century BC — someone who spoke God's messages to the ancient nation of Israel during a time of deep spiritual unfaithfulness. But before God gave him words to speak, He gave him a life to live.

There are commands in Scripture that require strength — build an ark, face down Pharaoh, climb a mountain with your son bound for sacrifice. Then there's the command God gave Hosea, which didn't require physical courage at all. It required something far more excruciating: the willingness to be publicly humiliated in the most intimate aspect of his life, to become the town joke, to love someone who would make a fool of him.

"Go, take to yourself a wife of whoredom."

There are men who marry women in adult films and claim it doesn't bother them. Maybe it doesn't. But imagine the rest of the world knowing what your wife does for a living and with who. Hosea didn't have to imagine it.

We don't know what Hosea's life looked like before that moment. The Bible doesn't bother detailing his family line or even a single fact of his life before God called him, as if his story didn't truly begin until God shattered whatever peace he'd known.

The Bible records no discussion over the matter, but it's impossible to play the scene out in our heads and not picture Hosea asking God all kinds of questions and pouring out the concerns of his heart.

What we do know is this: Hosea obeyed. He chose Gomer and married her.

He brought her into his home. He gave her his name.

This tells us volumes about Hosea. You do not agree to do something so bold, so foolhardy in the view of society, unless you are absolutely convinced that God exists, that God is trustworthy, and that your supreme duty is to love, honor, and serve Him.

And for a while, perhaps it seemed like it might work. Scripture tells us she bore him, Hosea, a son. God instructed Hosea to name the boy Jezreel, which means "God scatters." The name was a prophecy of coming judgment — God would scatter Israel for their unfaithfulness.

Then she bore a daughter. God told Hosea to name her Lo-Ruhamah, which means "no mercy" or "not loved." It was a declaration that God's mercy toward Israel was exhausted.

Then came a third child, a son, whom God commanded be named Lo-Ammi — "not my people." The covenant was broken. Israel was no longer God's people.

The wording in Scripture is striking. The first child is described as born to Hosea. The second and third children are simply described as born to Gomer, with no mention of Hosea as father. This leads many biblical scholars to conclude that these latter two children were fathered by other men — the customers who paid for Gomer's services when she returned to prostitution.

Imagine the daily humiliation. Calling his daughter to dinner: "Lo-Ruhamah, come eat." Introducing his son to neighbors: "This is Lo-Ammi." Every time Hosea spoke their names, he proclaimed Israel's judgment. Every time someone asked about his children's unusual names, he had to explain that God had commanded it — that his own family was a living prophecy of divine rejection.

And all the while, the town knew. They knew Gomer had gone back to the streets. They knew those children likely weren't his. They knew Hosea was raising the sons and daughter of his wife's betrayal, giving them names that announced to everyone exactly what kind of household this was.

"That man is a fool and deserves all the abuse he gets," some would say. Others just looked at him with a vacant stare and a slow shake of the head.

After bearing three children, Gomer went back to the streets, back to the transaction, back to the men who didn't love her but would pay for her.

This is where the story gets unbearable, because for the metaphor to work — for us to truly see what God was illustrating — Hosea couldn't just be going through the motions to follow God's commands. The living example of God's relationship with His wayward, disobedient people does not ring true unless Hosea loved Gomer deeply.

Hosea, whose heart was being torn apart in anguish, was a mirror image of God's distress over His disobedient Israelites.

Whatever his reputation had been before marrying Gomer, it must've hit rock bottom afterward.

God could have chosen any number of metaphors to describe this betrayal. He chose the most humiliating one imaginable and caused Hosea to live it out.

Just when the community thought Hosea couldn't fall any lower, he did. He didn't just wait for her to come home, no doubt believing she never would. He went to the auction block and re-bought the woman who had betrayed him and their children.

The price was fifteen shekels of silver and a homer and a lethek of barley — a strange, mixed payment that suggests Hosea didn't have enough silver to cover the full cost. Barley was a working-class grain, the cheapest he could offer. He scraped together what he could: some coins, some grain, whatever he had. The fool gave up his silver and even the grain needed to keep his family and livestock alive — all to buy her back.

It is the ultimate picture of a commitment that does not depend on feeling, mirroring the way God pursues us even when we're kicking and screaming, wanting nothing to do with the One who loves us most.

God's call to Hosea was unthinkable. When he obeyed, people thought he was crazy. But that doesn't mean God won't call you to do something practically unthinkable today.

Consider the adult children of neglectful and hurtful parents. God calls those children to forgive — not to pretend it didn't happen, but to release the grip of bitterness and extend grace to someone who didn't earn it. That command cuts against everything we believe about self-protection and fairness.

When you talk about forgiving the people who hurt you most, you'll have friends — including believing friends — whose initial reaction is to agree that some things are simply not forgivable. They will be like the people who thought Hosea was crazy or incredibly foolish.

Corrie ten Boom knew something about that. After surviving Ravensbrück concentration camp — where she watched her sister Betsie waste away and die — she came face to face with a former guard who had been especially cruel. He had come to faith and was asking for her personal forgiveness. Corrie was frozen. But she put out her hand and took his, asking God for the strength she didn't have. She described a warmth starting in her shoulder and moving all the way through to her hand. "I forgive you, brother," she said. "With all my heart."

That's an assignment right up there with Hosea being told to marry a prostitute.

Marry an unfaithful woman. Love her when she betrays you. Redeem her and bring her back home. It went against every instinct, every notion of self-protection, every principle of fairness.

But that's exactly the point. God was showing Israel — and showing us — what His love looks like. It's a love that pursues us when we're unfaithful. A love that forgives when we don't deserve it. A love that redeems us when we've squandered everything He's given us.

That's the lesson I've learned over the course of my life. God's assignments often seem wrong to our perception of justice, but they reveal something far more important — the depth of His love for people who don't deserve it, which includes every single one of us.

I taught high school for nearly 30 years. We never lost the house. But more importantly, I learned that God's uncomfortable assignments aren't punishments — they're investments in our character and becoming more Christlike.

That's what Hosea discovered. That's what Corrie discovered. And that's what you'll discover too, if you're willing to take the first terrifying step — whether that's walking into a Domino's with twelve dollars to your name or facing someone who once destroyed your trust.

9

Joseph and the Dirty Coke Bottles

I woke up one summer morning about the time my father usually went to work, but he hadn't left the house yet. My father was not a man to be late to anything, and certainly not work. So I was a little confused.

I could see down the hall that he was wearing the same grey Dickies work pants he wore ` single day. He had on his Red Wing boots, but today he was in no particular hurry.

I walked out into the kitchen to ask my mother why Daddy was still here. She said the contractor he worked for had no jobs, so he was probably going to be off for at least a few days.

That confused me, because it looked very much like he was getting ready for any other day of work. He walked into the kitchen, said goodbye to my mother, and grabbed his big gray lunch kit and a thermos of coffee. Then he went out the door.

No work meant no pay, and my father, a child of the Great Depression, wasn't going to sit idle.

That was back when soft drink bottles were made of thick glass and carried a cash deposit — you returned the empties to the store and got your money back.

While others tossed their empty bottles along the roadside, my father spent his days off combing the busy shoulders, gathering up the glass treasures he could scrub clean and trade for a nickel each.

He'd return home, drop the dirty bottles into an old bucket to soak off the grime, then settle on the back doorstep, scraping mud from the treads of his boots.

I remember one day in the early '70s when my father spent hours collecting bottles and came home to announce he'd earned a little over $2. The way he said it stuck with me, echoing in my memory even now.

There was no bitterness or disappointment in his voice—just a simple statement of fact.

Over the years, my thoughts about how to live in uncertain times have crystallized into an expression that may not be exactly original, but is nonetheless true:

When you don't know what to do, do what you know to do.

My father would never have used those words, but it was the way he lived his life.

Joseph never heard those words either. But he lived them more than 30 centuries ago in places my father couldn't have imagined.

His story starts a generation before he was born. His grandparents, Isaac and Rebekah, sent their younger son, Jacob, to Rebekah's brother, Laban, to find a wife among their own people.

When Jacob arrived, the first person he met at the well was Laban's daughter Rachel. Genesis tells us Rachel was beautiful, and it didn't take long for Jacob to know he wanted to marry her. He offered Laban seven years of labor for her hand.

But when Jacob's wedding night came, Laban pulled a switcheroo and brought his veiled older daughter, Leah, to Jacob's dark tent.

Jacob woke up the next morning to the ancient world's version of a bait-and-switch.

Remember Vacation's Clark Griswold going to the dealership expecting to pick up the Antarctic Blue Super Sports Wagon he ordered, only to find the Metallic Pea Family Truckster in its place?

When Jacob confronted Laban, the old con artist didn't even flinch. "It is not our custom here to give the younger daughter in marriage before the older one." It had the same shameless energy as Eugene Levy handing the keys to the ugly green behemoth to Clark and saying:

You think you hate it now, wait till you drive it.

Laban offered a deal: finish Leah's bridal week, work another seven years, and he could have Rachel too. Within days, Jacob had both wives under the same roof, and the sore that would define that household for decades was already festering.

Leah had son after son. She named her firstborn Reuben, which means "Look — a son!" — hoping it would make Jacob see her as something more than a distant runner-up to her sister.

Despite his great love for his wife, Rachel could give her husband nothing. The woman he had worked for for 14 years could not bear him a child. That had to be a galling competition. Rachel had her husband's great love, but her also-ran sister could pump out sons like a factory.

Then God remembered Rachel. Three words that carry decades of anguish behind them. She conceived and bore a son and named him Joseph, saying, "God has taken away my disgrace."

The miracle child of the favored wife, born into a house where every other son was a trophy in a war Rachel had been losing for years. Every brother in that house knew exactly where they stood the moment Joseph arrived.

It didn't help that Joseph brought reports of his brothers' bad behavior back to their father. Whatever they did wrong, Jacob heard about it from his favorite son. Genesis says the brothers hated him and could not speak a kind word to him. To them, he was their snotty little brother. Every conversation was through gritted teeth. Every exchange laced with venom.

When Joseph was seventeen, Jacob gave him a richly ornamented robe. It wasn't just a nice coat. The Hebrew term describes a long-sleeved, ornamental garment — the kind worn by someone who doesn't do manual labor. In a household of working brothers, it was the equivalent of a wearable will. Jacob announced to the family that this, the eleventh-born, would receive the authority and inheritance that, by custom, belonged to the firstborn. The brothers didn't hate Joseph because of fashion. They hated him because their father had just told them, without saying a word, that none of them could compete with his golden boy.

If you've ever watched Brad Garrett play Robert Barone on Everybody Loves Raymond, you know what it looked like inside that household. Robert spent the entire series knowing his mother preferred his brother and was unable to do a thing about it.

Robert summed up his whole life experience by saying, "Raymond's the one who gets the parade. I'm just the guy who follows the horses with the shovel."

Their father deeply loved Joseph, but just handed his older brothers shovels.

Then came the dreams.

Joseph dreamed that he and his brothers were binding sheaves of grain in the field, and his sheaf rose and stood upright while theirs gathered around it and bowed down. He told his brothers about his dream.

Let me engage in a little understatement and say their response was what economists would call sub-optimal.

Then he had a second dream — the sun and moon and eleven stars bowing down to him. This time, he told his father too. Even Jacob rebuked him: "What is this dream? Shall I and your mother and your brothers actually come to bow ourselves to the ground before you?"

Joseph was just a teenager, but he had a coat that made him a target and two dreams that made no sense to him. He had no burning bush, no angel, no voice from heaven telling him what any of it meant. All he had was a father's favoritism that painted a bullseye on his back and a pair of visions that, shared out loud, guaranteed that every brother despised him and wanted him gone.

What happened next would make sure they got their wish.

One day, Jacob sent Joseph to check on his brothers and the flocks — a journey of roughly fifty miles. When he arrived, they'd moved on to Dothan, another fifteen miles north. So Joseph kept walking.

Anyone who's ever watched someone with no experience get handed authority over people who've been doing the job for years knows exactly what those brothers felt when they saw that coat coming across the field. Of all the things they didn't want to see — rival shepherds, wolves, bad weather — nothing was worse than their kid brother, the supervisor, holding his clipboard and wearing the boss's coat, coming to file a report.

They saw him from a long way off. And the Bible says something that should stop every reader cold: they conspired to kill him.

This was not a crime of passion. They saw him in the distance, which means they had time — time to talk, time to plan, time to agree. This was a pressure cooker that had been building for years, and it was about to blow.

"Look, the dreamer is coming," they said to each other. "Let's kill him and throw him into one of these pits. We can say a wild animal devoured him. Then we'll see what becomes of his dreams."

They didn't know it and couldn't have imagined it, but what they were doing was the first step in seeing those dreams fulfilled.

Reuben, the oldest, talked them out of outright murder.

"Don't shed blood," he said. "Throw him into this pit," Genesis tells us Reuben intended to come back later and rescue Joseph. Whatever his motive — conscience or pragmatism — it bought Joseph his life.

When Joseph reached them, they grabbed him, stripped that hated robe off his back, and threw him into a stone-walled, dark pit.

Then they sat down to eat.

That detail sends a chill: a group of men leaves their brother for dead, then pauses for lunch as if nothing happened. Their hatred had simmered so long that tossing Joseph into a pit barely touched their appetite.

It was Judah who came up with an alternative that might have been a little more humane but also more cold-blooded. A caravan of Ishmaelite traders was passing through on their way to Egypt, and Judah saw an opportunity. "What profit is it if we kill our brother and cover up his blood? Let's sell him." The brothers agreed. They pulled Joseph out of the pit and sold him to the traders for twenty pieces of silver — the price of a common slave.

Then they took his robe, slaughtered a goat, and dipped the coat in the blood. They brought it to their father and, in what had to be one of the worst acting jobs in history, said, "Look at this — is this your son's robe? We're not really sure."

Jacob recognized it immediately and came to the quick conclusion that a wild animal had torn his beloved son apart and eaten him.

He tore his clothes and put on sackcloth, mourning his son for many days. He refused to be comforted, and not one of those brothers told the truth.

A father who had any awareness of how dangerous that household had become would have been suspicious. Jacob wasn't. He had spent years pouring favoritism on Joseph like gasoline, never once looking around the room to see the roaring fire.

The same blindness that led him to give the coat led him to believe the story about the coat.

Meanwhile, Joseph was in the back of a caravan, heading south toward Egypt. Just seventeen years old. No coat. No father. Sold by his own brothers into slavery, and all he had to hang onto were a couple of dreams that didn't make any sense to him.

Beyond that, God was silent.

The traders sold Joseph to Potiphar, an officer of Pharaoh and captain of the guard. Everything he had known — his father's house, his coat, his place at the table — was gone.

But being sold to Potiphar was about as good an outcome as Joseph could have wished for. This was a man of means, with a well-run household and experience leading other men. If you had to be a slave in Egypt, this was the place.

In terms of words and visions, God was silent, but He was anything but quiet in Joseph's circumstances. He had gifted Joseph with the skills he would need to be successful in whatever situation he found himself in, and in Potiphar's house, those gifts became visible fast. Joseph arrived knowing nothing — not the language, not the customs, not how anything in Egypt worked. And yet whatever he managed — whether in the house or in Potiphar's broader affairs — turned out remarkably well. Scripture says the Lord was with Joseph, and everything he touched prospered.

Genesis tells us that Potiphar saw that the Lord was with Joseph. Even though he was most likely a pagan, he knew there was something special about this young Hebrew slave.

Potiphar was so impressed with Joseph's skills that he eventually stopped managing anything. With Joseph in charge, Potiphar only had to concern himself with what was on the dinner menu each day. A teenage slave from Canaan, running the estate of one of Pharaoh's senior officers — not because of a résumé, but because God made it happen.

And then one day, Joseph's fortunes did a 180-degree turn.

Genesis tells us Joseph was handsome in face and form. The Bible doesn't often comment on people's physical appearance, but when it does, it's there for a reason. Potiphar's wife took special notice of Joseph, and there was nothing subtle about her intentions. Day after day she came at Joseph, and day after day he refused. His reasons were clear, and they came in a specific order. First, her husband had been good to him — Potiphar had trusted Joseph with everything he owned and withheld nothing except his wife. Second, what she was asking was a sin against God. Joseph led with the argument she might understand and closed with the one that mattered most to him. He was a man of absolute principle, and no amount of persistence was going to change that.

So Joseph did what the Bible tells us to do with sexual temptation — flee. He didn't try to change the subject or reason his way through it, he ran. But on this particular day, she grabbed hold of his garment, and he literally slipped out of it, getting away from her.

The scorned woman went to her husband with the garment in her hands and told a filthy lie, all to get back at the man she wanted but who would not submit to her advances. Listen to the words she chose.

"That Hebrew servant tried to grope me."

That. Dismissing him as irrelevant.

Hebrew. She spat out his ethnicity like a slur.

Servant. She wasn't referring to Joseph the way her husband saw him, but as a common slave.

Grope. She was saying he tried to violate her with his filthy hands.

She wasn't describing what happened. She was building a case with words chosen like weapons.

And it worked. Potiphar burned with anger, while I imagine his wife enjoyed a sadistic little smile. Joseph, a man who had done nothing wrong and everything right, was banished to prison.

But God wasn't finished. The same pattern that played out in Potiphar's house started again behind prison walls.

Genesis says the Lord was with Joseph and showed him kindness and granted him favor in the eyes of the prison warden. The warden put Joseph in charge of everything in the prison — every prisoner, every detail. Try to imagine a warden at a modern penitentiary trusting a slave turned inmate to run the place. In what world would that make sense? But that's exactly what happened.

Just like Potiphar, the warden stopped worrying about anything Joseph handled. The same words, the same outcome, the same invisible hand arranging circumstances for a man God had never spoken a word to.

Joseph did what he knew to do.

Some time later, Pharaoh's royal cupbearer and his royal baker both offended the king and landed in Joseph's prison. Joseph was assigned to attend to them, and Genesis uses a word worth noticing: he served them. Not a man leveraging authority over two disgraced officials, but a servant leader who actually cared about the people in his charge.

One morning, Joseph came to check on them and noticed something. Their faces were troubled. He didn't have to ask. He was running a prison, not a counseling service. But Joseph paid attention to the people around him, and he asked a simple question: "Why do you look so sad today?"

They told him they'd each had a dream the night before, and there was no one to interpret them. Joseph's response was immediate: "Do not interpretations belong to God? Tell me your dreams."

They wouldn't have shared those dreams with just anyone. The butler and baker opened up to Joseph because he had already shown them, day after day, that he was safe.

The cupbearer went first. Joseph interpreted his dream: within three days, Pharaoh would restore him to his position. Then Joseph asked for one thing — remember me. Mention me to Pharaoh. Help me get out of this place. It's the one moment in the story where Joseph advocates for himself — a quiet plea from a man who had been doing the right thing for years and was still sitting in a cell.

The baker, encouraged by the cupbearer's good news, shared his dream next, no doubt hoping for an equally cheery outcome. As they say in the investment world, past performance is no guarantee of future results. Three baskets of bread on his head, and birds eating from the top basket. Joseph didn't sugarcoat it. The three baskets were three days. Within three days, Pharaoh would have him executed.

Three days later, it was Pharaoh's birthday. He threw a feast for his officials, restored the cupbearer to his position, and in an oddly celebratory moment had the baker hanged. Everything happened exactly as Joseph had said.

And the cupbearer forgot about Joseph.

Two full years passed. The cupbearer went back to pouring wine for Pharaoh and never mentioned the Hebrew prisoner who had told him the truth when no one else could.

Two years. That's not an oversight. That's a man going to work every day with the king and never once thinking about the person who helped him in the worst moment of his life.

For most of us, two extra years in prison would seem like wasted time. But for God, it was right on schedule.

And Joseph kept running the prison.

Then, right on God's schedule, Pharaoh had some really weird dreams.

No, these were not run-of-the-mill dreams. These were the kinds of dreams we had that were so vivid and real that you woke up terrified, unable to dismiss them as just a dream.

In the first dream, he was standing by the Nile when seven fat, healthy cows came up out of the river and began grazing. Then seven gaunt, ugly cows came up after them, and the thin cows devoured the fat ones. Pharaoh woke up. He fell back asleep and dreamed again. Seven heads of grain, full and good, are swallowed up by seven sickly heads.

When morning came, Pharaoh's spirit was troubled in a way that his power couldn't fix. He summoned every magician and wise man in the kingdom. Not one of them could tell him what the dreams meant.

And that's when the cupbearer finally remembered. Two years late, but right on time.

He told Pharaoh about the Hebrew prisoner — how he and the baker had both dreamed in prison, how this young man had interpreted their dreams, and how everything had happened exactly as he said. The cupbearer restored. The baker executed. Every detail, precisely as the prisoner had called it.

They pulled him out of the prison, cleaned him up, and made him presentable. Then he was brought before the world's most powerful man.

Pharaoh told him, "I had a dream, and no one can interpret it. But I have heard that when you hear a dream, you can interpret it."

Joseph's response tells you everything about the man. Standing in front of Pharaoh, fresh out of prison, with every reason to seize the moment and make himself look indispensable, he said: "I cannot do it. But God will give Pharaoh the answer he desires."

Not me. God.

Pharaoh told him the dreams. Joseph didn't hesitate. The two dreams were one. Seven years of extraordinary abundance were coming to Egypt, followed by seven years of famine so severe that the abundance would be forgotten entirely. The thin cows devouring the fat, the scorched grain swallowing the full — it was the same message delivered twice because the matter was firmly decided by God and would happen soon.

Then Joseph did something nobody asked him to do. He didn't just interpret the dreams — he told Pharaoh what to do about them. Appoint someone to oversee the land. Take a fifth of the harvest during the good years. Store it. Build reserves. So that when the famine comes, Egypt survives.

Pharaoh looked at his officials. Then he looked at Joseph. The decision wasn't complicated. If God had shown this man what no one else in Egypt could see, then this was the man to put in charge. He told Joseph he would answer only to Pharaoh himself — and no one else in the kingdom would outrank him.

In a single day, Joseph went from prisoner to the second most powerful man in Egypt. Pharaoh put his own signet ring on Joseph's finger, dressed him in robes of fine linen, and placed a gold chain around his neck. He gave him a chariot and had men run ahead of him shouting, "Make way!"

If that were me, I'd be reeling from the emotional and mental vertigo of it all. But it seems likely that Joseph accepted the change and went to work immediately without the need for months of intensive psychotherapy. He had experienced a change as shocking as Keanu Reeves being ejected from the Matrix and welcomed to the real world. Except Morpheus never told Neo, "Oh, and we're giving you a new name, and you're married to the king's daughter now."

He was thirty years old. Thirteen years had passed since his brothers threw him in a pit. Thirteen years of slavery, false accusation, prison, and silence from God. And now he was standing in fine linen with Pharaoh's ring on his hand, in charge of feeding the entire known world.

The dreams he had when he was seventeen had not made any sense, but they were just starting to come into focus.

With Joseph in charge, the plan to store grain in newly constructed depositories was right on schedule. For seven years, Egypt produced in abundance, and Joseph made sure none of it was wasted. These had to be hectic, exhausting years — building an entire national reserve system from scratch for a famine nobody but Joseph believed was coming.

But personally, these were also sweet years. Joseph and his wife welcomed two sons — Manasseh and Ephraim. The names tell you where Joseph's heart was. Manasseh means "God has made me forget all my trouble and all my father's household."

Ephraim means "God has made me fruitful in the land of my suffering." You don't name your son "God made me forget" unless there's something you've been trying to forget. Joseph was healing, but the wound remained.

Then the seven good years ended, and the famine came — not just to Egypt, but to the entire region. And it was every bit as severe as Joseph had said it would be. The surrounding nations had nothing. Egypt had grain. And people began pouring in from everywhere to buy food from the man Pharaoh had put in charge.

Including ten brothers from Canaan who had to be uneasy at the thought of going to Egypt, where their brother, if still alive, was likely a slave. But still, what are the odds they'd encounter one slave in a land teeming with them?

They appeared before the governor of all the land and bowed their faces to the ground. They knew if things did not go well, they, their father, and their little brother back home were going to starve. None of them realized they were bowing before Joseph.

But he recognized them immediately.

His brothers had disliked him so much that they could barely look at him when he was young. But Joseph could never forget the faces of the people who abandoned him and sold him into slavery.

If we didn't know Joseph's heart, we might think at first that he was seeking vengeance. He spoke to them only through an interpreter. His tone was harsh. He accused them of being spies — men who had come to find Egypt's weaknesses, not to buy grain. They protested, stumbling over each other to explain.

"We are twelve brothers, sons of one man in Canaan. The youngest is with our father, and one is no more."

One is no more. They said it to a stranger's face without flinching. Twenty years of practice had made the lie smooth.

Joseph threw them in prison for three days. When he brought them out, he told them his terms. One brother would stay behind in custody. The rest could take grain home to their starving families. But they were not to come back unless they brought the youngest brother with them.

It wasn't vengeance. It was a test. Joseph needed to know whether these were the same men who threw him into a pit and sat down to eat, or whether twenty years had changed them. Would they sacrifice another brother to save themselves? Would they abandon Benjamin the way they abandoned him? He couldn't just ask. Men who sold their brother and lied to their father for two decades weren't going to confess to a stranger. He had to create a situation that would show him who they'd become.

What happened next told him something. Standing right there in front of the Egyptian governor, who they believed couldn't understand a word of Hebrew, they started talking to each other. "Surely we are being punished because of our brother. We saw how distressed he was when he pleaded with us for his life, but we would not listen. That's why this distress has come on us."

Reuben, the one who had tried to save Joseph years ago, added, "Didn't I tell you not to sin against the boy? But you wouldn't listen. Now we must give an accounting for his blood."

They had no idea Joseph understood every word.

He turned away from them and wept.

He composed himself, came back, and had Simeon bound and taken away in front of them. Then he sent the rest home with their grain — and secretly ordered his servants to put each brother's payment back in the top of his sack.

When the brothers stopped along the road and opened their sacks, they found the silver. They didn't feel relief. They felt terror. "What is this that God has done to us?" They were starting to believe that everything happening to them was connected to what they had done to Joseph. The guilt they had buried for twenty years was clawing its way to the surface.

They went home and told Jacob everything — the harsh governor, the accusation of spying, Simeon in custody, and the demand to bring Benjamin. Jacob's response was exactly what you'd expect from a man who had already lost Rachel and believed he'd lost Joseph. "You have deprived me of my children. Joseph is no more, and Simeon is no more, and you want to take Benjamin. All these things are against me."

He was wrong about every single one of them. Joseph was alive. Simeon would be returned. And sending Benjamin would be the final step toward saving his entire family. Jacob was standing in the middle of his rescue and calling it his ruin.

How many times have I done the same thing?

He refused. Benjamin was not going.

The famine didn't care about Jacob's refusal. The grain ran out. And Jacob, the man who had once wrestled with God, finally had to let go of the one thing he was gripping hardest. He sent his sons back to Egypt — with Benjamin.

When Joseph saw Benjamin, he had to leave the room again. He went into a private chamber and wept. His younger brother — Rachel's other son, the last piece of his mother — was standing right there. Joseph washed his face, composed himself, and came back out.

Then he did something that unsettled every brother in the room. He seated them at his table in birth order, from the firstborn to the youngest. The brothers looked at each other in astonishment. How could an Egyptian governor possibly know? And when the food was served, Benjamin's portion was five times larger than anyone else's. Joseph was watching. He was showing favoritism to Rachel's son — the same kind of favoritism that had started all of this — and waiting to see how they'd react.

They didn't react with jealousy. They ate and drank together. Something had changed.

But Joseph wasn't finished testing. He sent them home with their grain and had his personal silver cup hidden in Benjamin's sack. Before they'd gone far, Joseph's steward caught up with them. The sacks were searched. The cup was found in Benjamin's bag.

It was the final test — and the only one that truly mattered. Twenty years earlier, these brothers had been given a chance to protect Rachel's favored son, and they had thrown him in a pit instead. Now they were being given the same choice. Benjamin was caught with stolen property from the governor of Egypt. They could walk away, go home to their father, and let Benjamin take the fall. They could save themselves the way they'd saved themselves before — by sacrificing the favorite.

Judah stepped forward.

The same Judah who had said, "What profit is it if we kill our brother? Let's sell him" — that Judah — now stood before the governor and delivered a speech that may be the most remarkable transformation in the Old Testament. He told the governor everything. Their father's grief. The old man's love for Benjamin. The promise Judah had personally made to bring the boy home. And then he said words that would have been unthinkable from the man who sold Joseph for twenty pieces of silver:

"Please let me remain as your slave in place of the boy. Let him go back with his brothers. How can I go back to my father if the boy is not with me? I cannot bear to see the misery that would come upon my father."

The man who had once traded one brother's life for profit was now offering his own life to protect another.

That was the answer Joseph had been waiting for.

He couldn't hold it any longer. He ordered every Egyptian out of the room. And when it was just the brothers — just the sons of Jacob, alone in a room in Egypt — Joseph broke.

He wept so loudly that the Egyptians outside could hear him.

And then he said five words that shattered twenty years of silence:

"I am Joseph. Is my father still alive?"

His brothers couldn't answer. They were terrified. The brother they had sold into slavery was the second most powerful man in the world, and they were standing in front of him with nowhere to run.

Joseph said it again. "Come close to me." They came closer. "I am your brother Joseph, the one you sold into Egypt."

And then — instead of vengeance, instead of punishment, instead of everything they deserved and expected — Joseph told them something that reframed every moment of suffering he had endured for the last twenty years:

"Do not be distressed and do not be angry with yourselves for selling me here, because it was to save lives that God sent me ahead of you."

Not you sent me. God sent me. He said it three times — as if they needed to hear it again and again before it could sink in. This was not your plan. This was God's plan.

The dreams had come into focus. The sheaves were bowing. And the dreamer was saying — Don't be afraid. This was always the plan.

Joseph sent for his father. When Jacob arrived in Egypt — an old man who had spent twenty years believing his son was dead — Joseph rode out to meet him in Goshen. He threw his arms around his father and wept for a long time. Jacob said, "Now I am ready to die, since I have seen for myself that you are still alive."

Joseph settled his family on the best land in Egypt, provided for them during the remaining years of the famine, and ensured they had everything they needed. The boy who had been stripped of his coat and thrown in a pit was now clothing and feeding the very people who put him there.

Years later, when Jacob died, the brothers panicked. With their father gone, they feared Joseph might finally take his revenge. The buffer was removed. There was nothing stopping him.

But that was not in Joseph's heart. These were different brothers. He had tested them and watched Judah offer his own life for Benjamin. The men standing in front of him were not the men who had sold him.

Joseph told them again: "You intended to harm me, but God intended it for good, to accomplish what is now being done — the saving of many lives."

It was the last time he needed to say it.

Before Jacob died, he adopted Manasseh and Ephraim as his own sons, giving them equal standing with his other sons. That's why there is no tribe of Joseph in Israel — there are tribes of Manasseh and Ephraim instead. The coat had promised Joseph the double portion. The pit was supposed to destroy it. God delivered it anyway.

While in prison, Joseph made one attempt to better his circumstances — he asked the cupbearer to remember him. When it didn't work, he went back to running the prison. We never hear of him complaining to anyone about the injustice he'd been dealt.

No bitterness. No campaign. No list of grievances.

In every room he was placed in — a mansion, a prison, a palace — he thought about what he could do, not what had been done to him.

I have had a great many times in my life when I didn't know what to do. But in those paralyzed moments, I come back to just doing what I can do. Each little thing is like finding another empty soda bottle along the road.

My father never heard of Joseph. But they lived the same way.

Joseph proved it's enough.

10

Ananias and the Six-Foot Banana

About ten years into my teaching career, I was assigned to teach AP Government and Economics. AP, or Advanced Placement, courses are college-level classes taught in high school. Students who pass the national exam at the end of the year can earn actual college credit before they graduate. Now, the government didn't worry me. I had an extensive academic background and a lifelong personal interest in how the wheels of power turn. But AP Economics? That was a different animal entirely.

I had spent years teaching standard Economics and knew I was a solid teacher. But stepping up to AP felt less like switching horses and more like leaping from a gentle, coin-operated pony outside a grocery store straight onto a bucking mechanical bull—or maybe even the real thing.

That summer, I traveled to Rice University for a week of intensive training. Surrounded by seasoned teachers and a master instructor, everything made sense—at least in that safe, collaborative bubble. But knowledge has a way of evaporating between the cool comfort of a summer seminar and the heat of a Monday morning in late August. Alone in my classroom, thirty sharp-eyed students filing in, all expecting me to be the expert, I felt the weight of solitude settle in.

There are two kinds of AP Economics. Macro covers the economy as a whole: GDP, unemployment, inflation—the full forest. Micro focuses on how economic principles affect individuals and businesses—the bark on a single tree. With a business background, I chose Micro. I understood the details because I'd lived them. It was a start.

That first year teaching microeconomics, I was convinced I was letting my students down. I pictured our brightest kids, the pride of the school, crushed by dismal exam scores—and me, right there in the wreckage with them. But when July arrived, and the results came in, I was floored: they had outperformed both state and national averages. For a veteran AP teacher, maybe that's routine. For me, it felt like a triumph.

It was like a rookie manager whose team was expected to lose over 100 games but instead finished 83–79—a surprising victory.

After a few years, I left my school to work with at-risk students in my home district. I entered expecting to help struggling students but found that I learned just as much from them. After watching many overcome immense adversity to graduate, I felt called to start the AP Macroeconomics program at a new school, guiding their very first senior class.

While the prospect of starting this new program was initially thrilling, as the reality of the task set in, my excitement gradually gave way to growing anxiety—and then to outright terror.

This was my "Whole Forest." Economics, the Federal Reserve, gross domestic product, and stagflation were all new terrain. I didn't know the landscape. As the summer approached, my fear of dishonoring this shiny new school and letting down these students grew into a mountain. I tried to "weasel out" of it. I told the administrators, repeatedly and with great "magnanimity," that if anyone else wanted the class, I would gladly step aside. I called it humility; God knew it was cowardice.

I prayed for God to give the cup to someone else, but He didn't. I stayed. I taught twenty-three consecutive semesters of AP Macroeconomics, becoming something like a grizzled old trail boss on countless cattle drives from South Texas to the railheads in Kansas.

Then came the afternoon of the monthly faculty meeting. It was probably my sixth or seventh year of teaching AP Macro. Every month, in the faculty meetings, they announced a "Teacher of the Month" winner. Most of the time, awards like that are given to excellent teachers of elective courses. In those classes, students build half-scale models of modern aircraft carriers, complete with nuclear reactors, only waiting for fissionable material.

To my utter shock, I heard my name called as the Teacher of the Month. I had my laptop out working during the meeting, and it took me a minute to stand up and get down to the front of the auditorium. There, the principal handed me a Teacher of the Month certificate and, in a touch of true high school glory, a six-foot-tall stuffed banana.

As I turned to head back to my seat, clutching my oversized Chiquita, the principal stopped me. He then read a letter he had received from the College Board, the international organization that administers the Advanced Placement program worldwide. The letter stated that 127,000 students had taken the AP Macroeconomics test the previous year, but only 57 students worldwide had achieved a perfect score.

I had taught one of those 57 students.

The letter congratulated the school and stated that the student's perfect score was a sign of the "outstanding instruction taking place on our campus."

I stood there, speechless, clutching a ridiculous stuffed banana while the principal read a letter about the quality of my instruction — the very instruction I had tried to "weasel out" of because I was sure I would fail. It taught me that my lack of faith was no match for God's insurance policy. I had tried to negotiate a retreat, but God was busy planning a ticker-tape parade.

Which brings me to Ananias. He was a nobody in Damascus, a quiet believer doing quiet work, until God handed him an assignment involving a man named Saul. Now, Saul wasn't just a guy with a bad attitude; he was a one-man wrecking ball for the early church.

Before we can look at Ananias's hesitation, we have to respect the dossier he was holding. We've "Sunday-schooled" Saul of Tarsus into a leather-bound author of the New Testament. But to the believers in Damascus, he was a state-sponsored predator. Saul was a brilliant, high-ranking member of the Sanhedrin with the full weight of the law and the temple guard behind him. He had already stood by and offered approval to the men who stoned Stephen, the church's first martyr. He had systematically dismantled the church in Jerusalem, dragging men and women from their homes. Now, he had traveled 135 miles with official extradition papers to do the exact same thing in Damascus.

When Ananias said, "Lord, I have heard from many about this man," he wasn't just being cautious. He was reminding God that this man's entire mission was to erase everything Ananias held dear. He was a "most wanted" man being asked to hand-deliver himself to the bounty hunter.

We aren't told exactly how Ananias reacted to God's instructions in that moment. The Bible gives us the facts, but it doesn't always give us the heart rate. However, if it were me, I think I'd become something like Bob Newhart in that situation.

I imagine Ananias starting that conversation with the enthusiasm of a man who just won "Disciple of the Month."

"Yes, Lord! You need me to run an errand? I'm your man. Whatever you need, I'm already halfway out the door."

And then God drops the bomb: "Go down the road to a house on Straight Street, and meet a man named Saul."

A weighty Newhart-style pause ensues.

"Uh, yeah... Okay... Sure... Y-You know, there are quite a few Sauls in town, Lord. It's a popular name. Good, sturdy name. Which Saul were you thinking of, specifically?"

"The one from Tarsus."

"Ha! Ha-ha... oh, Lord, You really had me there for a second. That is a good one. 'Saul of Tarsus.' The guy whose hobby is hunting people like me? That's rich. You always have such a great sense of humor."

Then comes the silence on the other end of the line. The kind of silence that only happens when you realize the Creator of the Universe isn't joking.

"Y-y-y-you're serious? Saul? You mean the Saul? The 'arresting and killing everyone', Saul? Uh-huh... I see. And you want me to go to his house. Right. Forgive me, Lord, but it sounds like you're telling me to go into a cave and poke the bear, is that it?

No, no, I'm sure you have a plan... It's just that, well, Lord, I've heard reports about this guy. Bad reports. Very... stabby reports. And you want me to just knock on the door? Yes, I hear you.

A-A-A-AND who are you sending with me?

Nobody? With all due respect, God, don't you think this is a Delta Force or SEAL Team 6 situation?

Uh, you want me to go alone?

Lord, have you considered sending Peter? You know Peter. He's... well, he's a tough guy. We call him Chuck Norris in sandals. He's got muscles, a sword, and just the kind of volatile temperament needed for this job.

Yes, Lord, I know you chose me specifically, but...

I understand, Lord. But you know I'm more of a 'Sunday school teacher, fellowship hall, pray over the cupcakes and punch' kind of disciple. Are you sure you don't want the guy who cuts ears off for this one?

...OK, Lord. I'll go. I just wish I had a Kevlar tunic to wear for this house call."

But the joke ends the moment Ananias hangs up the phone.

The Bible tells us, "Ananias went and entered the house." It's one of the most underrated sentences in scripture. It doesn't say he went because he felt brave. It says he went. Every step he took toward Straight Street was a victory over the sheer, logical "No" that his circumstances screamed at him.

God wasn't asking him to run a difficult errand; He was asking him to walk into a room and publicly pronounce his faith to a man already covered in the blood of his friends. He was walking toward a potential trap, a likely death sentence, and the personification of the early church's greatest fear... Every step toward the house of Judas was a victory over the fear and apprehension he refused to let control him. When he finally reached the house, he saw Saul, not as the monster of the reports, but as a blind, praying man weakened from not having eaten in three days.

In that moment, Ananias didn't hesitate.

He didn't lead with a lecture. He reached out, placed a hand on the shoulder of the early church's greatest fear, and said two words that changed the history of the world:

"Brother Saul."

Ananias's fear stemmed from who Saul had been. The moment he placed his hand on that shoulder, the information gap closed, and the fear dissolved. But not every fear works that way. Some fears are based on facts that haven't changed at all, where the danger is real, current, and verified, and no amount of new information makes it any less so.

A few weeks had passed since Ananias knocked on that door.

Saul had been baptized, had eaten and had regained his strength. And then, with the same relentless energy he had once aimed at destroying the church, he began preaching in the Damascus synagogues that Jesus was the Son of God. Saul — who would become known by his Greek name, Paul — was now a target.

The reaction was predictable and swift.

The Jewish authorities who had sent Saul to Damascus with extradition papers now felt something far more personal than betrayal. Their most effective weapon had defected, worse, he had joined the other side and was now dismantling their arguments from the inside. The governor serving under King Aretas had also joined the effort, stationing men at every gate in the city wall. Acts 9 tells us the Jews were watching the gates day and night. Paul's own account in 2 Corinthians adds that the governor's soldiers were there too.

This was not a vague threat. It was not an old reputation or an outdated report. It was an organized, two-front manhunt with the full weight of both religious authority and regional government behind it. The city had walls. The walls had gates. The gates had armed men. And every one of those men was looking for the same person.

The disciples in Damascus faced a fear unlike Ananias's. His fear dissolved the moment he saw a blind, praying man rather than a predator. These believers had no such revelation waiting for them at the end of the street. The danger they faced was exactly as dangerous as it looked.

They had a choice. They could step back, keep their heads down, and let Paul fend for himself. Few would have blamed them. The man had spent his career hunting people exactly like them. His conversion was only weeks old. And the people now searching for him were the same people who would come looking for anyone who helped him.

They didn't step back.

What they came up with was not sophisticated. There was no elaborate Great Escape tunnel, no bribed official, no forged documents. Someone had a house built against the city wall, common enough in ancient Damascus, with a window that opened out over the other side. And so the disciples took a basket, put Paul in it, and lowered him down the wall in the dark.

Think about that for a moment. The man who would go on to write nearly half the New Testament, who would plant churches across the known world, who would stand before kings and governors and Caesar's own household, his great escape involved being folded into a laundry basket and dangled over a wall by his friends while armed soldiers patrolled below.

God is not always theatrical about these things.

This is where many of us get confused about faith and fear. We read the Old Testament, and we see God parting the Red Sea, the Egyptian army bearing down, with nowhere to run, and

God tells Moses to stand still and watch. Spectacular, undeniable, it requires nothing from the Israelites but stillness and trust. And we think that's what obedience in the face of real danger always looks like. We wait for the sea to part.

But look at how God responds to real danger elsewhere. When Herod's soldiers were hunting the infant Jesus, God didn't tell Joseph and Mary to stay in Bethlehem and trust Him to blind the soldiers. He told them to pack up and flee to Egypt. When Jezebel put a death warrant on Elijah, God didn't call down fire from heaven. He told Elijah to hide by the Kerith Ravine. In both cases, the danger was mortal and verified, and God's answer was a road and a canyon, not a miracle. Strategic obedience is still obedience. Practical deliverance is still deliverance. You just don't get to choose which kind God hands you.

The disciples in Damascus didn't get a parting of the sea. They got a basket and a dark night and a prayer that no one was looking up.

What God asks in every case is the same thing: obedience anyway. Not obedience because you can see how it will work out. Not obedience because the danger has been neutralized. Obedience in the dark, over the wall, hoping no one is watching.

The disciples who lowered Paul over that wall didn't know what was waiting on the other side. They didn't know if soldiers were positioned outside the walls as well as inside. They didn't know if Paul would land safely, slip away undetected, or be captured the moment his feet touched the ground. They knew the danger was real and the plan was improvised, and God had not handed them a guarantee.

They lowered him anyway.

Sometimes God doesn't part the sea. Sometimes He hands you a basket and says, "Trust Me anyway."

Here is what I want you to see before we leave this city.

Ananias walked down Straight Street because God told him to, even though every bit of information he had said it was a death sentence. He placed his hand on the shoulder of the church's greatest enemy and said two words that changed the trajectory of human history. Then he stepped back into his quiet local ministry and probably never fully understood what he had set in motion.

But follow that thread forward. The man Ananias restored became the man the whole city wanted to capture. And the believers who helped Paul escape over that wall, many of them almost certainly part of Ananias's own community, people he had prayed with and broken bread with, acted with the same raw, unadorned courage their brother Ananias had shown weeks earlier.

Notice, though, that their fears were entirely different in character. Ananias walked toward a man whose danger had already been neutralized; he just didn't know it yet. His fear was based on accurate information that was no longer current. The disciples at the wall faced no such revelation; their danger was real, present, and fully operational, and no new information was going to change that. And the fear I faced in front of that first AP Macroeconomics class was neither of those; it wasn't about danger at all. It was the fear of my own inadequacy, the quiet dread of being exposed as someone who didn't belong at the front of that room. Three entirely different fears. Three entirely different circumstances. But the obedience they required looked exactly the same.

One man's obedience on Straight Street rippled outward into a community of people who knew how to be brave when it mattered. That's how it works. Courage is contagious. Obedience teaches obedience.

And none of it, not the restored sight, not the transformation, not the escape, not the letters to the Corinthians and the Ephesians and the Romans that you have read your entire life, none of it happens if Ananias decides the risk is too great and stays home.

He didn't stay home.

Neither did the disciples with the basket.

Neither did I. I stood in front of my first AP Macroeconomics class feeling certain I was about to fail in spectacular fashion. I taught anyway.

The fears were different. The assignments were different. The baskets were of different shapes.

But the obedience looked exactly the same.

Here's how I think about it. I wouldn't be afraid to walk through the most dangerous neighborhood in America if I had a team of Army Rangers flanking me on both sides. My circumstances haven't changed, the neighborhood is still dangerous, but my assessment of the risk changes completely based on who is walking with me.

Now suppose trouble finds us anyway. Thirty or forty armed marauders step out of the shadows. Maybe the Rangers raise their weapons and dispatch every one of them before I've fully registered what's happening. Or maybe the Ranger commander grabs my arm, points to an alley on the right, and says, *"Get in that dumpster and don't move. "*Two completely different experiences. One is spectacular; one smells terrible. But in both cases, I walk out the other side alive because of who was with me, not because of anything I brought to the situation.

How much more should our fear dissolve when we recognize that God Himself accompanies us wherever He sends us? The neighborhood doesn't change. The assignment doesn't change. But who is walking with you changes everything.

Here's something worth knowing. When Paul writes in 2 Timothy that God hasn't given us a spirit of fear, the Greek word he uses is deilia, which doesn't mean fear at all. It means cowardice. God never promised to remove the fear. He promised not to leave us paralyzed by it. Ananias proved the difference.

And so does God's question to you.

Whatever street He is asking you to walk down, whatever basket He is handing you, the question is the same one Ananias faced on the road to Straight Street. Not "Can I guarantee how this ends?" Not "Do I feel brave enough?" Not "Is the risk acceptable?"

Just this: Will you go?

11

Peter and the Unopened Snickers

When I taught AP Economics, I taught students who were extremely smart, very hard-working, and very hard on themselves when they didn't succeed. Some of these kids cannot get past failure. All they can see is flashing red lights, and they're convinced something is about to run them over. I know how counterproductive that is. If your focus is on kicking yourself, it precludes making any progress toward getting better. The two things cannot happen at the same time.

So I had to do a lot of what I came to call talking economics students down off the ledge. And what worked was this: I would drop my voice down very low, very soft, and talk to them in the calmest voice I had with as much compassion as it could carry.

I remember one young lady in particular. It was after school, and almost all of the students had cleared out except for a few seeking tutoring. We were sitting at desks facing each other, going over a quiz, she had scored a 52 on, and I watched as heavy tears fell from her eyes and splattered out on her desk.

My usual response in that kind of situation was to go into protective Dad mode. Despite looking like a teaching giant, I have a very soft heart, and nothing activates it faster than seeing tears in the eyes of one of "my kids." I grabbed a jumbo student-tears-sized box of Kleenex, a bottle of cold spring water, and 3 or 4 fun-sized candy bars.

Students would always use the tissues and usually drink some of the water. When the student opened and ate the candy, I knew I had won the battle against discouragement.

At first, those things only did so much, but they were just the start of my rebuilding effort. Then I told her this grade didn't mean anything. It never happened — I'll take it out of the gradebook. Then we can take it down to the office and shred it. We could even set the shreds on fire outside.

But, I joked, before we started the pyrotechnics, we ought to go through one of the questions she missed — we're not going to worry about the whole test, just one problem, step by step. Her response was a tiny, hopeful smile. She wiped her eyes, and we were actually talking.

We worked through one problem. A few minutes in, she said — oh, I didn't know that. She got the answer. Then I gave her one similar to it, and she worked through it and got it right.

After she got those two right, she ripped off the wrapper of a miniature Snickers and took a bite.

The next week, she made the highest grade on the AP unit test I gave — not just the highest in her class. The highest grade in any of my classes.

Now here is a devastating confession.

I truly believe in the grace and mercy I offer students and the grace God offers sinners, but I have a very difficult time offering that grace to myself.

Peter was about to find out exactly what that feels like.

He had been following Jesus and his arresting party at a distance since Gethsemane — close enough to watch, far enough to hide. They brought Jesus to the courtyard of the high priest's house, and Peter slipped in and stood by a charcoal fire to warm himself while the interrogation went on inside.

Twice already, Peter had been recognized as one of Jesus' followers, and he denied it both times.

About an hour passed. Then a third person — a relative of the man whose ear Peter had cut off in the garden — pressed in. Certainly, this man was with him. He's a Galilean.

Peter's first two denials were quick and flat dismissals.

But with this identification, something malignant deep in his heart erupted. Peter was no longer just denying Jesus in words; he was invoking God's name in doing it.

May God strike me dead if I'm lying.

And immediately, while he was still speaking, the rooster crowed.

And then, Luke tells us, the Lord turned and looked straight at Peter.

I have thought about that look for a long time. There is something in it that cuts differently than anger or even disappointment would. If Jesus had looked away — if He had

been too occupied or too broken by His own night to notice —
there would be a kind of mercy in that. Peter's failure could
have gone unwitnessed. Private. Between him and the dark.

But Jesus turned and looked.

Not only had Peter denied Jesus 3 times, but Jesus had been
close enough to see it happen — just as he had predicted at the
Last Supper.

Then, he went out of that place and wept bitter tears — the kind
of sobs that take over your body and overwhelm every other
impulse.

He couldn't shake it — that look wouldn't go away, and Peter
feared it never would.

Peter had not always been this man weeping in the dark.

He had been there the day Jesus looked at him and said you
will be called the Rock — before Peter had done a single thing
to earn the name.

He had been in the boat when the nets came up so full they
nearly sank two boats, and he had fallen to his knees on the
deck and said go away from me, Lord, I am a sinful man.

He had stepped out of a boat onto open water in the middle of
a storm because Jesus said come — and for a moment,
impossibly, he had walked on water.

He had stood at Caesarea Philippi and given the answer no one
else would give: you are the Messiah, the Son of the living God.

He had seen things no human being had ever seen, and he still
blew it.

And in the worst possible way.

I know how it feels to fail God spectacularly, and the thoughts that won't leave me alone when I do.

I can tell a student to stop kicking herself, and mean every word of it. I can walk her through it step by step and watch her come out the other side.

But I cannot do one word of it for myself.

I know students must move beyond failure and extend grace to themselves so they can go forward.

But knowing it for others doesn't make me know it for myself.

When I have blown it with God, my first instinct is to get as far away as possible. How can I face him when I have failed and failed and failed? When I have ignored the faithfulness he has shown me and treated his word like unread junk mail? The dread of having to face God hangs over me like a sword. I can run, but I can't escape the dread. That's a pattern I faced more than once as a teacher.

I was a jealous teacher, and in the best possible way. Jealous of my class time and intolerant of anything that stole it.

The speaker crackled to life just as I was launching a lesson."Teachers, please pardon this interruption."My students would later describe my physical reaction as a life-sized balloon deflating. That became a running joke that only they found funny.

Two minutes of announcements. Then silence. I gathered them back, rebuilt the setup, and the speaker came on again. Then a third time before the period ended.

I sent an email to my principal — a nice guy, a reasonable boss, and a former classroom teacher — attaching a news article about a state rule limiting interruptions. I asked about our school's compliance.

His reply was short. He wondered why I was taking instruction time to send that email. And then, come to my office after school. I want to talk to you.

Those seven words were a millstone around my neck for the rest of the day. I limped through my remaining classes, dawdled after the bell, and finally made my way down the hall.

His door was open. He greeted me with a warm smile — not like a shark anticipating its dinner. He walked me through circumstances I hadn't known about and hadn't bothered to ask about before firing off that email.

I had spent an entire afternoon carrying a loathsome millstone when the actual burden was but a pebble.

For Peter, his millstone felt very real and heavy.

After the fire in the courtyard, after the denials, after the bitter tears, and an inability to forget Jesus looking at him, he stumbled through the next couple of days with a dead weight clinging to him. The freedom from the burden was still ahead.

Then, on Sunday morning, Mary Magdalene came running to Peter and John and reported that the stone had been rolled away and that the tomb was empty. The men then raced to see it.

John stopped at the tomb's entrance and looked in. And Peter, being Peter, ran right in — finding the burial wraps folded, the body gone.

Then Jesus appeared. First to Mary. Then, to the ten disciples gathered behind locked doors. Then, a week later, to the same group with Thomas present. Peter had seen him again. He had seen him twice now. Jesus was alive.

But every appearance had been to the group. Jesus had stood among them, shown his hands and his side, spoken to them together.

Peter was no doubt overjoyed, but he must have also dreaded the day he would have to face Jesus alone.

Then one day Peter announced, "I'm going out to fish," and the other 6 men who had fled from Jesus in fear, each carrying a similar burden, joined him.

These were men who had worked together for years — easy conversation, shared jokes, the comfortable rhythm of men who knew each other well. On this day, I imagine their talks were quieter with more questions than answers.

Carrying the weight of what they'd done, and unsure what came next, they did the one thing that was second nature to them — but they fished all night and caught nothing.

Early in the morning, a man they didn't recognize stood on the shore and called out to the men in the boats.

"Got any fish?" he asked in a friendly voice.

Their reply was a curt "No." But I guess having thrown nets out all night and pulling them up empty robbed them of their eloquence.

The stranger on the shore told them to throw their net off the right side of the boat. He said they'd find fish there.

Professional fishermen who have just spent an entire night finding nothing don't usually take casting advice from a man on the beach. But they threw it anyway. What was the risk? They were about to row in without so much as a goldfish.

Then something happened that was surprising — and then, almost immediately, wasn't. The net filled so fast and so full that they couldn't haul it in.

It was John who recognized Jesus, telling Peter, "It is the Lord!"

Once again, his reaction was classic Peter. As soon as he heard John identify Jesus, Peter jumped in the water and worked his way 100 yards up to the shore while the others came in with the boat, towing their full net.

Jesus called out to the men and told them to bring some of the fish they had caught. Scripture tells us that Peter ran to the boat to help drag the net ashore.

Which means that after swimming 100 yards to get to Jesus, Peter kept his distance once he arrived.

This was Peter acting in character — impulse carrying him to one extreme and then the other. It was the same man who told Jesus he would never wash his feet, and then thirty seconds later asked him to wash his head and hands too. Maximum in one direction, then maximum in the other, with nothing in between.

The shore was no different. He couldn't stay in the boat. He couldn't quite close the last few feet either.

When Jesus called out for some of the fish, Peter had something to do with his discomfort. He turned and ran to the boat — close to shore by now — to help drag the net in.

Not far. But far enough.

Jesus told them to come and eat. And the men who had worked through the night came to the fire hungry and sat down.

John records something that sounds strange at first. He tells us that none of the men asked who Jesus was — and then in the very next breath tells us they knew it was the Lord.

Those two sentences feel like odd bookends. If I were writing about running into my pastor at a restaurant, I wouldn't tell you I didn't ask his name. You already know I know him. The fact that John bothers to record the absence of a question tells you the question was there.

Something about Jesus in that moment made the recognition land slowly. Not with doubt exactly — but with the kind of knowing that arrives before you're ready to say it out loud. He didn't look like the man they had spent 3 years with. But the voice, the authority, the fish where there had been none — everything else about him said it was him. Close enough to be certain. Different enough to hold your breath.

Nobody asked. They all knew.

After they had eaten the grilled fish and some bread Jesus had baked, it was time for the conversation Peter had been dreading — but knew was coming.

The conversation was like an inevitable trip to the dentist. You have put it off as long as possible, but now your tooth is making your life miserable.

Peter was far from the high priest's courtyard now. But one thing was the same — the charcoal fire.

It was around a charcoal fire, surrounded by strangers, that Peter had denied Jesus three times. And now here was the same fire, surrounded by his closest friends.

This conversation was going to be just as public as the denials.

When the last of the breakfast was finished, Jesus turned to Peter.

Peter had been waiting for this since the courtyard. And now here it was — no more net to drag, no more fish to count, no more reason to keep his hands busy and his eyes down.

I wonder what Peter saw when Jesus looked at him. Because I think he may have been reading that face the way I have sometimes read an email — arriving at it already expecting a certain tone, and finding exactly what I expected, whether it was there or not. If Peter came to that moment convinced that Jesus saw a failure and a coward, that is probably what he saw looking back at him. Confirmation bias is not a modern invention.

What Jesus actually said was not what Peter was bracing for.

"Simon, son of John — do you love me more than these?"

As he asked it, I imagine Jesus gestured at the boat, the brothers, the nets, the whole familiar life. Do you love me more than the stuff in your life?

Peter answered carefully. "Lord, you know that I love you."

Not more than these. Just — you know that I love you.

Jesus said: Feed my lambs.

Then he asked again. "Simon, son of John — do you love me?"

Again, Peter answered. "Lord, you know that I love you."

Feed my sheep.

Then the third time. And this time something in the question landed differently — harder, deeper, in a place Peter hadn't let anyone touch since the courtyard. Jesus asked him a third time, and Scripture tells us it grieved Peter deeply.

Three denials. Three questions. Jesus is going all the way to the bottom of the wound. The third question was what hurt. Not punishment — precision. The same way a doctor sometimes has to press on the wound to know if it has healed. Peter needed to feel the full weight of it one more time, not to be crushed by it, but to be freed from it. The pride that had made him boast at the table —even if all the others fall away, I never will— that pride had to be addressed, not just the denials.

Peter answered a third time. "Lord, you know all things. You know that I love you."

And Jesus said: feed my sheep.

Three times asked. Three times answered. Three times charged. What Peter had done in the dark around one fire was publicly, deliberately, completely reversed around another.

He had come to that beach expecting a three-count indictment and guilty verdicts.

What he got was an assignment and grace.

When it was over, I think Peter finally understood what he had been reading wrong since that night. The look in the courtyard hadn't been condemnation. It had been this — the same eyes that were now looking at him across a charcoal fire on a beach in the early morning, already seeing not the man who had failed, but the man who would feed the sheep.

It was the same thing I tried to tell that young lady sitting across from me with tears on her desk. This is not about what went wrong. This is about what comes next.

God's great mission for Peter came after the apostle's colossal and very public failure. But failure isn't disqualifying. It's just a part of every believer's résumé.

So what went on Peter's résumé after the beach?

Fifty days after the resurrection, Peter stood up in Jerusalem on the day of Pentecost and preached the first sermon in the history of the Christian church.

The man who couldn't hold up under a servant girl's question held up under the weight of a crowd — and 3,000 people came to faith that day.

When the authorities dragged him before the Sanhedrin — the same council that had condemned Jesus — Peter stood in the same room where his Lord had been sentenced to die. He looked them in the eye and told them plainly that salvation came through Jesus Christ alone.

The most powerful religious court in the world told him to stop talking. He told them he couldn't. Not wouldn't. Couldn't.

The man Jesus had named the Rock before he'd done a single thing to earn it — became exactly that.

That résumé was built on the other side of the beach. Every entry on it traces back to a charcoal fire and a question asked three times.

I seriously doubt Peter was ever completely free of the memory of that courtyard, just like those of us who have lost our parents can never fully forget our last moments with them.

Even though I can't fully forget the times I've failed God, that doesn't mean I have to agree with the interpretation Satan is trying to push into my head.

His trick has never been reminding me that I failed — I can do that fine on my own.

His trick is convincing me that the grace I'm clinging to like a lifebuoy in a raging sea is the illusion.

I know exactly what I would say to Peter if he were sitting across from me at a desk with tears hitting the surface between us. I'd slide the box of tissues over, set a bottle of water in front of him, and tell him we're not going to worry about the whole night — just one step. Just what comes next.

And I think I'm finally starting to understand that when Jesus met him on that beach, that's exactly what He was doing. Not reliving the failure. Not piling on the weight. Just putting one simple question in front of him, and then another, and then another — until Peter was back.

I've helped many students take that step.

I'm still learning how to take it myself.

12

God, the Spinach Can and Me

Like countless small children, I idolized my father. I couldn't wait for him to get home from work at the end of his day. He wasn't precisely the Norman Rockwell image of a father, but he had no equal to me.

As I got into my teenage years, I realized things about my father that troubled me. Most notably, there were constant reminders that my family didn't have many things that the neighbors did. At the time, I didn't understand why. I just found out we didn't have them and learned it was pointless to ask for them.

Despite the miserably hot, humid summers, we never had air conditioning in our house in Pasadena. Instead, we had an old attic fan in the hallway that wouldn't even start on its own. For years, we had to turn on the wall switch and then, using an old broomstick, nudge the fan blade in the right direction before it would start moving air around our little house.

We also never had a color television. Instead, my father would buy a "big" 19-inch black-and-white model, and we'd wear it out before spending money on a new one. Before touch controls and remotes, TVs used big, clunky mechanical tuning knobs. When the plastic knobs finally broke from years of use, my father would set a pair of pliers by the television so we could still change channels.

As a teenager, I always felt uneasy and more than a little embarrassed when new friends came to our house. We weren't the Clampetts, but I knew we were awkwardly different and lived far behind the times.

I'd hear of my friends' family vacations and creature comforts that were utterly foreign to me. I saw friends getting new coats each year when it turned cold, but I often wore hand-me-downs from my older brothers. I remember being self-conscious about wearing a six or seven-year-old coat that looked even older. Any protest I might make fell on deaf ears, so why bother? We knew that one of my father's cardinal rules was not buying something new when the old was still serviceable.

As I moved into my teens, my dad's whole attitude grated on me. Why wouldn't he get with the times? He had a steady job, and Lord knows we never spent much money. Why did we have to live like we were practically penniless?

Every Saturday, my parents would leave the house with grocery ads and coupons in hand and spend three hours driving from store to store, buying only what was on sale. Going to a single market like Lewis and Coker or Weingartens to buy the week's groceries was out of the question. Each of those stores might have some good specials each week, but they were otherwise, in the words of my father, "higher than a cat's back."

The further I went into my teenage years, the farther I felt from my father. By the time I was 20, I was married, and two years later, I had a son of my own. Over the next ten years, my wife and I would have another son and a daughter.

I would like to say that getting older and having children closed the relationship gap with my father, but it didn't make much difference. I was on my own and could buy some of the affordable luxuries my little family wanted. Still, whenever I went to my parents' house, it felt like I was walking backward in time.

Visiting my parents' sweltering house in the summer sometimes brought back the old contentious feelings. Deep down, what genuinely bugged me was a strong belief that my father thought I was stupid.

In my mind, he regularly reinforced this notion throughout the years. Each fall, the first time the temperature dropped to 40 degrees, I could always count on a call from my father. He'd ask, "You got any antifreeze in your car, son?"

That always irritated me. Didn't my father know that water froze at 32 degrees, not 40? Why didn't he think I had a brain in my head?

That was a minor gripe, but more evidence of his apparent belief that I was a child who needed his hand held at every busy intersection of life.

Why couldn't he understand that I was a responsible man on my own?

I was not so blunt with my father on those calls, but my attitude was certainly more dismissive of him than was proper for a son talking to the man who had raised him.

I carried that attitude right into my thirties. I was going to figure out my own life, on my own terms, without anyone holding my hand — least of all my father. And then reality arrived, the way it has a habit of doing.

At 32, I enrolled in college when we already had a mortgage and three kids. Going to school year-round would take me just over three years and four months to finish, and each of those months was a struggle. We were often a mortgage payment or two behind, and our grocery budget was meager.

I quickly realized I was a capable student. I made the dean's list each semester in my first two years of college, but that was a given since I had a perfect 4.0 GPA. Had the school given me grades for being a great family provider during those days, I would have been on the verge of suspension for my entire college career.

At this point, I needed my father again, but I was a grown-up and independent, so I would never ask for his help. It turned out that I didn't need to ask.

During my early college years, it became common for my parents to show up at my house with bags of groceries. There would be whole chickens, hamburger meat, bacon, eggs, and coffee. After they left, we'd find cans and cans of fruit and vegetables that my father, the penny-pinching shopper, had bought on sale — sometimes as cheap as six cans for a dollar.

There is little doubt in my mind that my family survived my college years because of these grocery deliveries.

We were incredibly grateful for the help, and it came countless times in those years. My father once said he didn't give me money because he knew he could buy a lot more food with a dollar than I could.

Of that, there was no doubt in my mind.

In the spring of 1994, my father was diagnosed with terminal pancreatic cancer. The doctors gave him about nine months to live, and that estimate proved to be very accurate.

As he wasted away that summer and fall, I worked as many hours as possible while taking a full load of classes. One of my classes was a history of the Great Depression. For the first time, I got a close-up view of the lives of people living in that dark, unsettled time.

My father was not the type to talk a lot about his childhood, but I knew he never finished school. Tidbits of stories come to mind about him and his entire family working in the fields daily so they could have food on the table each evening.

Every Christmas, my father would make sure we had apples, oranges, and walnuts in the house. He would also buy odd-looking cut rock candy each year — the garish kind that looked like quaint antiques compared to my day's Sugar Babies and M&Ms. He told my brothers and me more than once that his Christmas present as a boy would usually be an apple or an orange along with a few nuts or a little hard candy.

I hate to admit it now, but I did not give such stories much credence. Dad's Christmas tales were just more of the "when I was your age, I walked five miles to school in the snow" kind of stories kids mock.

In the time I had left, I spent many more days with my father and asked him about his life. I could ask the questions then, or the answers would remain a mystery forever.

At one point that semester, the weight of my father's life experiences came crashing down on me. Like the denouement of a mystery novel, his words and actions finally made sense to me. The scales fell from my eyes — but this only happened in the last few months of his life.

I would sometimes hold my dad's hand, like when I was a little boy, knowing that soon I would never be able to do that again.

My father died on January 4, 1995. He was 76 years old.

Many months after he died, I was reorganizing the canned goods in our pantry and came across a can of Allens brand Popeye spinach. When I moved it to a different shelf, I spotted something odd on the label. What I saw gave me a cold chill.

My father had penciled the word "NEW" on the label. The can must have been part of one of his grocery care packages from my college years. It was evident that fifty-five years after the Great Depression ended, my father had been stockpiling food — just in case.

Looking back, I now see that my father was like a man who had been badly burned as a child and carried the scars quietly for the rest of his life. Those scars were not easily visible, but they showed up in every careful, frugal decision he made.

I remember him going to work as an electrician on cold, rainy days when he was sick. More than once, he badly cut his hand while stripping insulation from wire, got it stitched up, and went back the next day. Words were not his primary way of saying I love you. The antifreeze calls were. The grocery bags were. The penciled word on a spinach can was.

Today, I smile when the weather turns cold in the fall. I almost expect the phone to ring. I would welcome that call more than I can say — just for the chance to tell him: *I get it now, Dad. I really get it.*

I know that will never happen. But I keep the spinach can where I'll see it every day.

Here is what I've been thinking about for most of this book.

Noah didn't know he was saving the human race. He knew he had an assignment that made no sense to anyone watching, and he built anyway. Hosea didn't know his broken marriage would be read by millions as the most vivid portrait of God's love ever written. He knew he had been asked to do something that defied every reasonable instinct, and he obeyed anyway. Joseph didn't know the pit was the first step to the palace. He knew the bottom had fallen out of his life, and he had no choice but to keep moving through the dark.

They were all looking through the windshield.

The rearview mirror on our lives is always much clearer than the windshield when we're trying to see the road ahead. My father's antifreeze calls looked like condescension through the windshield. The grocery bags looked like charity. The frugality looked like deprivation. It took decades, a Depression history class, a dying man's hand in mine, and a penciled word on a spinach can before the mirror got clear enough to see what had actually been there the whole time.

Love. Just love. In every form, he knew how to give it.

If you are somewhere in the middle of your own impossible assignment right now — something that looks like foolishness to the people watching, something that has cost you more than you expected and returned less than you hoped — I want to suggest something. The mirror isn't clear yet. You're still looking through the windshield at a road you can't fully see.

But somewhere down that road, there may be a pantry. And in that pantry, on a shelf you haven't reached yet, there may be a spinach can with your name on it.

And when you find it, you'll get it.

You'll really get it.

Thank you for reading. If this book meant something to you, I'd be grateful if you left a review on Amazon — it makes a real difference for a first-time author.

You can find more of my writing at allenreding.com, or reach me at allenwrites7@gmail.com

About the Author

Before becoming a full-time writer, Allen spent nearly three decades teaching economics in Texas, helping students understand the difference between economies that create wealth and those that spread misery.

He and his high school sweetheart, Becky, have been married for 45 years. By God's grace, they've raised three grown children, all married now, and two young grandsons who are walking encyclopedias on obscure dinosaur species—and who keep their grandparents humble and exhausted.

Allen graduated from the University of Houston at the ripe old age of 36. He and Becky live in the Bay Area of Houston, just down the road from NASA's famed Mission Control.

When he is not writing, and sometimes even while he is, he and Becky can be found aboard cruise ships. They savor coffee side by side as they watch the endless blue water and soak in the gentle ocean breeze.

He wrote this book because he kept asking himself whether being able to write meant he was meant to write for God. That question opened the door to the Bible's unlikely servants—the people who wrestled with their own inadequacy, yet still found themselves in God's hands.